Instructor's Resource Manual
for

Foundations
A Reader for New College Students
Second Edition

Virginia N. Gordon
The Ohio State University

Thomas L. Minnick
The Ohio State University

WADSWORTH

THOMSON LEARNING

Australia • Canada • Mexico • Singapore • Spain • United Kingdom • United States

Printed in the United States of America
1 2 3 4 5 6 7 05 04 03 02 01

0-534-52432-X

For more information about our products, contact us at:
Thomson Learning Academic Resource Center
1-800-423-0563

For permission to use material from this text, contact us by:
Phone: **1-800-730-2214**
Fax: **1-800-731-2215**
Web: **www.thomsonrights.com**

Asia
Thomson Learning
60 Albert Complex, #15-01
Albert Complex
Singapore 189969

Australia
Nelson Thomson Learning
102 Dodds Street
South Street
South Melbourne, Victoria 3205
Australia

Canada
Nelson Thomson Learning
1120 Birchmount Road
Toronto, Ontario M1K 5G4
Canada

Europe/Middle East/South Africa
Thomson Learning
Berkshire House
168-173 High Holborn
London WC1 V7AA
United Kingdom

Latin America
Thomson Learning
Seneca, 53
Colonia Polanco
11560 Mexico D.F.
Mexico

Spain
Paraninfo Thomson Learning
Calle/Magallanes, 25
28015 Madrid, Spain

CONTENTS

Preface

Preface

Freshman seminar courses (of more or less the sort for which we designed this textbook) have been taught in American universities for well over a century. Many of these courses were developed out of a recognition of the unique needs of first-year college students. A history of such courses would reflect the changing purposes of higher education as it has evolved into a uniquely American institution. These purposes were influenced by the changing economic and social needs of a growing country, as well as by a recognition—one that is still emerging nationally—of the special concerns new students face in their transition to college life.

The amazing diversity of approaches and formats of the freshman seminars reflects the diverse character of the institutions that teach them. In a national survey of programming for the freshman seminar courses by the National Resource Center for the Freshman Year Experience, five types of freshman seminars were identified:

1. Extended orientation courses which emphasize college survival or student success topics;

2. Academic seminars with uniform academic content across sections which are often interdisciplinary or theme-oriented;

3. Academic seminars on various topics which focus on the academic interests of the faculty member teaching the course;

4. Professional seminars which are taught within professional schools or specific disciplines; and

5. Basic study skills seminars which are tailored to the needs of underprepared students.

Foundations: A Reader for New College Students was developed to support these various types of courses. The second edition has been enlarged to accommodate changes, especially in technology, that have swept across American institutions of higher education, and revised based on the experience of classes of classes that used the first edition. The nine themes which compromise the new edition apply universally to first-year students regardless of age or type of institution. The readings introduce new students to many of the issues they will confront during life in and after college. They are especially relevant to courses based on interdisciplinary or academic themes, they can be used with basic study skills seminars that stress the importance and practice of reading, and they require varying levels of reading skill and so suitable essays can be assigned at whatever level the instructor deems appropriate.

Since the themes of these nine units represent general concerns of college freshman, the text can also complement materials which provide a local orientation. The versatility of **Foundations 2/e** makes it a valuable tool for increasing the skills of reading and critical thinking. The vocabulary items and the discussion questions after each essay can assist instructors in enriching the quality of discussion on may critical issues that confront and challenge new students. The themes are common to the content of many existing freshman seminar courses which have provided a time-honored structure for generations of college students.

This instructor's resource manual is intended to offer assistance in presenting the ideas of the diverse authors represented in **Foundations** and for facilitating student discussions of these ideas. **Whether you use Foundations 2/e as a primary text or supplemental one**, this collection of readings should stimulate the thinking of beginning students as they embark upon a critical period of intellectual and personal growth.

Foundations 2/e is an outgrowth of a freshman seminar that the authors have been associated closely with for almost three decades; many of the essays from this collection have been pretested by more than 100,000 students! These readings (and, be assured, Dear Reader, several essays the authors rejected) have been used to challenge and stimulate student thinking on questions that run like a repeated pattern through the lives of first-year students: How can I successfully make the transition from high school to college? What career should I select to insure a comfortable life? How cam I plan for my future?

Each unit in the anthology draws together thinking from several points of view on a question that students should be asking themselves. We anticipate that different campuses and different instructors will emphasize these nine questions in different degrees. The discussion questions that follow each reading in the anthology (and that we have tried to answer from our own perspective in this manual) are included as supplements to your own ideas about the essays, as do our "suggested activities" after each reading. While some instructors may have a course framework in which all the essays in a unit (or in all units) may be assigned, others will select the few from each unit which represent their own campus discussions on the topic, or that seem particularly appropriate to a given class of students. We have also found it helpful, from time to time, to vary the assigned essays in order to retain a personal freshness with the course material.

THE VALUE OF A COLLEGE EDUCATION: WHY AM I IN COLLEGE?

The intent of the readings in Unit I is to challenge first year students' thinking about the purpose of higher education. Because of the historic roots of higher education and its continuing purposes, many of these readings ask students to consider the following question: "How compatible are my personal reasons for enrolling in college are with the ideal of becoming 'an educated person'?"

Many students enter college with little knowledge or understanding of the tremendous opportunities the college experience offers to their psychological, spiritual, social, and intellectual growth. The readings, therefore, focus on how students can take advantage of these opportunities.

The first readings look at the college experience from philosophical and practical perspectives. The last reading provides a brief history of how American higher education has evolved from colonial times to its present form. Students' awareness of the progression and changing purposes of higher education can add to their commitment and appreciation for the possibilities their college experience can offer.

UNIT 1 READINGS

The Lure of Learning
William Bennett

Many students can resonate with Bennett's reason for being in college ("to land a good job and make money"). Some may have high expectations for being taught by the kind of professor that Bennett describes. The central theme in this reading, however, is to encourage college students to be open and questioning so that many learning opportunities are not by-passed and that many practical lessons for living may be learned from exposure to "life's enduring questions."

This essay can lead to a discussion of faculty members' roles in the higher education enterprise and the students' impressions and experiences thus far with college teaching. It can also lead to a discussion of the rationale for general education requirements and how studying the great thinkers in many disciplines can relate to the resolutions of problems confronting business, politics, science, and other areas of life.

Discussion Questions

1.   How did Bennett and his fellow students initially react to their philosophy class? How did their reactions change?

They didn't think the questions of justice and right or wrong should occupy their time. They were soon caught up in the "serious enterprise of raising and wrestling with questions." Students might be asked if they have ever had the experience of initially disliking a course only to find, after enduring, that it was one of the best they have taken. What made them change their opinion? What did they learn about themselves in the process?

2.   What does Bennett ask undergraduates to do in order to expose themselves to the same wonders of learning that he enjoyed?

They should not only expose themselves to all the great works written in their discipline (major) but try to absorb the best that has been thought and written in every discipline. Do students place too much emphasis on the courses in their "major" at the expense of not appreciating the relevance or the important knowledge that can be acquired from their other courses?

3.   According to Bennett what gives each campus its own "special genius"?

The relationship between teachers and their students. It is important to be exposed to professors who can "bring to life" the subject they are teaching. Students can share some experiences with "great teachers" that they have worked with in the past. What qualities did these teachers have? What was special about their relationships with these teachers?

4.   What should students find at college in addition to good teaching?

The time and opportunity to explore the great works that tell how "other civilizations have grappled with life's relentless questions" and to read great works outside their major. How many students actually do this now? Is it as important as Bennett indicates? What "great works" have they read that they would recommend to their friends?

5.   What does the college experience do for a future career, according to Bennett?

The college experience can prepare students for a better and happier life since they will be better prepared to deal with problems as they come in any career-related situation or life endeavor. Discussion could center around student opinions about how a college education will help them in their future role as a worker, beyond the specific work-related knowledge and skills they acquire from the curriculum (e.g., extracurricular activities).

Suggested Activities

1.   Ask students to keep a journal of personal reactions to the assigned readings in this text and to write about what new insights are generated in their thinking. The questions asking for their personal reaction to each essay can be used as a stimulus for their writing.

2.   Ask students to describe their "ideal faculty member." How can students' academic expectations be different from those of faculty? How might they be the same?

3.   Invite a seasoned faculty member or a panel of faculty from a variety of disciplines to class to describe how they selected their profession, and how it affects their life style and their personal goals. Provide the opportunity for students to question the faculty.

The Difference between High School and College
Jack Meiland

Many students have "heard" that the rigor of academic coursework in college is greater than in high school, but they aren't sure of what these differences will be or how they might react to them. Meiland's unveiling of these differences can help new students understand the subtle but important expectations of the coursework in which they are involved.

Discussion Questions

1. What, according to Meiland, do high school students assume about high school teaching?

   That they are responsible for memorizing "facts" and that the teachers are "authorities" since they have mastered factual information. Do students agree with Meiland's assessment of high school instruction? What other roles are expected of high school teachers that aren't of college teachers?

2. What does a college course expect that is different from high school?

   College work requires a different kind of intellectual activity. The student will learn not only what is "currently believed," but also the basis on which the information is believed. College work "consists of discussing and examining the basis of current beliefs." Not only must the student learn the material but must critically examine and evaluate it. Have students found this to be true of their experiences in the classroom so far?

3. What does Meiland mean by "a rational justification of belief" when referring to college course work?

   College teachers not only impart information but want students to defend it on the basis of its rationality. The student is to believe the information on the basis of reason, not just take the word of the "authority." The student's task is to investigate the rationality of the information that is presented. Have students experienced this approach to learning in any of their classes? What has been the expectation of the teacher in this situation? Should teachers demand participation in class discussion? Should participation be rewarded? If yes, how?

4. What is the difference in material being presented by an "authority" versus material presented for "rational justification"?

   The shift from one method to another has implications for how the material is presented. Rather than being presented as factual, the material is open to conjecture and must be supported by argument and evidence. Are students finding this "shift" a difficult task? How does this affect the way they study for the course? How does it change their responsibility for what transpires in the classroom?

5. Why is "fact" in high school treated as "belief" in college courses?

   All "facts" must be questioned. While they are believed now, they may turn out to be wrong in the future. When they are treated as theories, they must be supported with evidence and placed against other theories which might be better.

Suggested Activities

1.   Ask students to take one fact they learned in high school and state it as a theoretical question (e.g., that the North "won" the Civil War). How does this change their thinking about this "fact"? What evidence supports their belief that this fact is true?

2.   Ask the students to discuss which method they prefer: being taught facts by an "authority" or being asked to examine the basis for, and evaluating facts after they have learned them. Where does each method lead them intellectually?

A New Debate is Joined Over an Old Question:
Is College an Investment or an End in Itself?
James Cicarelli

This essay can challenge students to consider the purpose of higher education and what they want personally from the experience. How can one measure how successful a college education has been? By how students have been intellectually enriched? Or by how successful they are in the job market? Would it be more feasible to measure it right after graduation or ten years out of college? Or at the end of life?

Discussion Questions

1.   What do advocates of the "value-added" philosophy consider to be the worth of a college education?

      The "value-added" approach measures the effectiveness of the education through the amount of quantifiable knowledge obtained. Through "outcomes evaluation," the store of knowledge that each student received can be measured (by nationally standardized tests, for example).

2.   According to Cicarelli, how do "traditionalists" view higher education?

      Traditionalists view college as a place where students learn to "appreciate their cultural heritage, hone their skills in critical thinking and communication, and . . . transform themselves . . . into decent and caring citizens."

3.   What are the differences between a specific career-oriented education and a general, liberal arts education?

      A career-oriented education provides a body of knowledge that the student must master in order to perform the task associated with a specific occupation. A general, or liberal arts education provides students with "skills that transcend specific jobs and can be . . . applied to any occupation."

4.   How does Cicarelli distinguish between romanticism and realism? Which do you think is the better view? Why?

      The traditional approach can develop "free-thinking" citizens who are willing to question authority rather than "accepting it blindly." A romantic sees the "value-added" approach as a way to force a certain curricula on everyone, thus not allowing for individualism. A realistic approach, however, understands how important it is to allow students to choose the institution that best serves their needs and values.

5.   Does Cicarelli think the question of "value-added" assessment will be resolved? How?

      He says it is difficult to tell how the debate will be resolved. The type of institution will determine which approach is used. Those with no national reputation and few resources will probably use the value-added philosophy. The better-known institutions will probably stick with the traditional view. The colleges with "average" students, reputations and resources will determine the outcome of the debate.

Suggested Activities

1.   After describing the two points of view on the purpose of higher education presented in this reading, ask the students to divide into two groups according to their belief. Ask each group to list reasons for their

side of the debate and present them to the other side. After the discussion, ask if any changed their minds and why they changed.

2.   Obtain (or create) a checklist of reasons why students enroll in college (e.g., because their parents expect it, to obtain a better job, for the social life). Ask students to check the reasons they are enrolled and to prioritize the reasons they have given. Lead a class discussion on the reasons students give and how these can influence their attitudes toward the two philosophies described by Cicarelli.

An Uncluttered Perspective: The True,
the Beautiful, and the Good
Howard Gardner

Some educators think that a college curriculum should teach specific content areas, and there have been many debates about what content should be included. These ongoing debates, often described as discussions over the "canon" of what should be taught, have been highly political in recent decades. Howard Gardner, instead of focussing on content (for example, literature by "dead white males" versus books by male and female authors from many cultures), identifies three "realms" of human experience—truth, beauty, and morality. Then he argues that " 'an education for all human beings' needs to explore in some depth a set of key human achievements captured in the venerable phrase 'the true, the beautiful, and the good'."

Discussion Questions

1. What is the purpose of education, according to Gardner?

"In the end," Gardner says, "education has to do with fashioning certain kinds of individuals—the kinds of persons I (and others) desire the young of the world to become. I crave human beings who understand the world, who gain sustenance from such understanding, and who want—ardently, perennially—to alter it for the better." This is Gardner's statement of the purpose of education. In addition, he says that " 'an education for all human beings' needs to explore in some depth a set of key human achievements captured in the venerable phrase 'the true, the beautiful, and the good'." He believes that the "masterpieces," the "pinnacles " of human achievement as objects of study are interesting in their own right and that understanding these great examples makes students into better citizens.

2. What does Gardner mean when he says "the range—the summits, the valleys, the straight and meandering paths—of what other humans have achieved . . ." Is his metaphor from geography useful?

Gardner is continuing a comparison with education as training for living in the world. He summarizes this in the sentence, "Such citizens [those who want always to alter the world for the better] can only come into existence if students learn to understand the world as it has been portrayed by those who have studied it most carefully and lived in it most thoughtfully...." He is therefore comparing the geography of the earth to the geography of the intellect—which has summits, pinnacles, straight and meandering paths. This general way of speaking uses concrete images (mountains, roads) to explain abstract ideas (mountains = important intellectual achievements, and meandering paths = unexpected and sometimes hard to find ways to a final intellectual outcome). Concrete comparisons can help the reader understand complex ideas.

3. Gardner chooses Darwin's theory of evolution as his example of "the True." Explain why this is a controversial choice.

As Gardner himself reports, one out of every two Americans believes that the theory of evolution is false, and even 20 percent of science educators think it is false. This choice for an example of "the True" shows which side Gardner is on. Readers can confidently deduce from Gardner's position that he opposes the notion that public schools should be required to teach creationism as a legitimate way to explain the history of our species in the world.

4. Gardner explains that his selection of examples is based on his cultural framework. Using the examples as your clues, characterize Gardner's personal cultural background.

A person's cultural background may not be the same as his or her ethnic or national background. For example, an Asian American who was raised in a Buddhist household with at least one parent who is a scientist might have received early training in classical music and love Mozart. Such a person might also be gravely troubled by the history of the Holocaust. So this hypothetical individual might be ethnically Asian American and spiritually identified with Buddhism--but culturally Western in outlook.

That is to say, it is not possible from the clues in this essay to identify Gardner's ethnicity. However, it is reasonable to deduce that he has a traditional "western" education, believes in the scientific method and verification, and values classical western music (Bach, Beethoven, Brahms, and above all, in his case, Mozart). He is also open to ascribing high intellectual value to the achievements of cultures other than his own.

Suggested Activities

1. Have each member of the class ask one person from outside the class to complete a brief survey--a simple three-part questionnaire that asks a respondent to identify one example of the True, one of the Beautiful, and one of the Good. Then bring these answers together in a class setting and compare them. An interesting twist on this activity is to ask half the class to talk with somebody younger than themselves and the other half to talk with somebody at least ten years older than themselves.

2. What is the reverse of the True, the Beautiful, and the Good? It can be fun and informative to ask students to identify examples of the genuinely False, Ugly, and Evil. What characteristics define these three antitheses to Gardner's thesis?

American Higher Education: A Brief History
William H. Halverson

This essay outlines how American higher education evolved from colonial times to the present. The English and German influences on our present system are also described. Most students are not aware of the uniqueness of the American system or how it has changed since its inception. Discussion can center around how the history of higher education reflects the evolving history of our country's economic, social, and political milieus. Students may want to contrast their life as a college student today with the life of students in colonial times, after the Morrill Act in 1862, or at the beginning of the 20th century.

Discussion Questions

1. Where did American higher education have its origins?

    The earliest form of American higher education was modelled after the English universities, Oxford and Cambridge. The German influence was felt in the late nineteenth century as some institutions were formed for the purposes of research rather than to emphasize instruction. A direct result of the German influence was the formation of the graduate school.

2. Why were the colonial colleges established?

    They were established "to ensure that the colonies would be supplied with literate and humane intellectual leaders, especially clergymen." The early colonists realized that education was needed to furnish the type of citizens who would be leaders in both the church and government.

3. What were the first curricula like?

    The first curricula were designed to "educate gentlemen." This was the model brought to the new world by the English settlers. Courses included Latin, Greek, Hebrew, ethics, politics, mathematics, botany, and theology. Later, more emphasis was placed on mathematics and science and a broadening of exposure to English language and literature. French (and other foreign languages) was also added by some.

4. What significant changes were made in the post-Revolutionary period?

    The number of colleges increased dramatically. The "classical education" was seen as ill-suited to the practical needs of a growing nation. Science and technology were needed so courses such as chemistry, geology, economics, law, medicine and other professional studies were added to the curricula. While a core of common courses was retained, each student selected other courses that filled each individual's needs and goals. During this time "teacher education" was also instituted. Colleges for women were established and some colleges began admitting both men and women.

5. What significant event happened in the late nineteenth century? What impact did it have on higher education even to today?

    Congress passed the Morrill Act in 1862. This act authorized grants of land to each state so that at least one college in each state fulfilled the goals set forth by the Act. In addition to scientific and classical studies, the inclusion of additional teaching of agriculture and mechanical arts was specified. The land-grant concept made higher education accessible to not only the wealthy, but to the industrial classes as well.

Suggested Activities

1. Ask groups of students to research one aspect of the history of higher education and give an oral report to the class. Provide a list of resources and some possible topics from which they can select.

2. Invite to your class an alumnus who graduated at least twenty years ago to describe what it was like to be a student on your campus at that time.

3. Ask students to interview a faculty member who has been at your college for twenty years or more. Provide a list of possible questions for them to use during the interview. The questions might include the faculty member's perspectives on the history of your institution and how it has changed during their tenure.

WHAT CAN I EXPECT FROM COLLEGE, AND HOW WILL I CHANGE?

The readings in the second unit focus on areas of concern that many first year students experience. Students often feel apprehensive about their new environment. Many traditional age students are looking forward to the idea of being "on their own." Older students wonder about their ability to "keep up," and experience some doubts about their ability to meet the challenge of academic coursework.

The readings in Unit II can help students recognize their adjustment concerns are not unusual. They can also be reassured that what they are experiencing is "normal" and that they are not the first or only students who wonder if they will be able to cope with new demands in a new environment.

Discussions centering on the developmental tasks through which students pass can help them understand that they will experience some common changes and growth. Older students can understand how they may need to rediscover some of the feelings they experienced at another time in their lives--e.g., wanting the teacher, who represents authority, to provide more structure, wanting to achieve intellectual competence, needing to develop a career purpose.

UNIT 2 READINGS

Two Million Futures . . .
Wesley R. Habley

Relying on statistical generalizations, Habley discusses some of the characteristics of the entering classes of the opening of the new millenium. For example, they share a number of similarities: they show increased levels of stress over previous entering groups, they report less commitment to social activism, and that they smoke and drink less than previous recent groups. While Hadley emphasizes that "these reports may accurately describe a group but do not necessarily describe any single individual who is a member of that group," he says these generalizations can be useful. They provide a "template" of demographic descriptions.

Several demographic themes define the newest college students. They join a rapidly growing world which will require more thoughtful resource management than previous generations. They will not share a concept of "family." And soon, no one is likely to be a member of a majority ethnic group. Changes in the economy, technologym, the political environment—all these will affect the entering generation of students, along with major national and international events. Habley cites Waco, Columbine, the Oklahoma City bombings as examples.

In spite of all their similarities, Habley concludes that each of the two million students annually starting college brings "a unique set of characteristics and experiences . . . and each seeks meaning from the college experience in a unique and personal way."

Discussion Questions

1. What does it mean to say that "demography is destiny"? Is it true?

The slogan, "demography is destiny," expresses the belief of some experts on the future that the changes they can predict will rule the lives of those who will live in the future. On the contrary, Habley believes that demography will play a role in the life of every new student, but he denies that "demography is destiny." Instead, he argues that individuals bring very different personal aspirations and experiences to their own futures, and therefore that no futurist can predict in more than general ways.

2. A familiar topic in many discussions about college is the four-year degree plan. Why do you suppose that students often do not finish their college degrees in four years?

   The answer to this question varies, of course, from student to student. First, we should note that the model of the four-year degree is often held up as though it were usually the case in the past that most students finished in four years. In truth, at many colleges (especially larger ones), many students never completed a degree. And for many years (the 1960s through 1973), the military draft insured that most students (then mostly male) stayed on track or went into one of the armed services.

   Now students may elect to take longer than four years in college in order to study abroad, to participate in one or more career-related internships, or for many other positive reasons. Students have more majors and programs to choose from today than forty years ago, and students today feel greater freedom to change their minds about academic or career directions. Finances play an important role: many students pay some or all of their college expenses, and they may need to "stop out" every so often to replenish their money supply. Finally, some undergraduate programs are not designed for completion in four years.

   In our view, here is the real issue: it is not shameful (as some seem to think it is) to take longer than four years to complete a degree.

3. Are you part of "the majority culture" of your home town or city? Describe it and how you do, or do not, fit in.

   Students will have to define "majority culture" in their own ways. Ethnic majority/minority issues come first to mind, but for some, the majority in their town or high school was second-generation immigrants, or Roman Catholic, or Jewish. Some students will come from dominantly first- or second-generation college going backgrounds. Others will arrive on campus from well-to-do communities where nearly every high school student owned a late model car. Others will describe rural, agricultural backgrounds. Once that "home town majority culture" is defined, students can relate their ties to it. Some may have been part of it but are ready to change, even to rebel. The discussion on this topic can reveal the ways in which even students who look very much alike are different in important ways.

Suggested Activities

1. Do any of the students disagree with the demographic patterns that Habley identifies? Ask the class to take sides on issues he points to—like our changing family models, or the end of a dominant majority culture. For each issue, put students from different sides into small groups and let them generate a list of "pros and cons," the arguments that help them to define their differences on these points. If you have a local issue that adds focus to one of Habley's points, all the better. You might, for example, ask about the need for bilingual instruction in some places with a large Spanish-speaking population.

2. Students from an earlier generation in college were able to talk about the ways in which Pearl Harbor or the war in Vietnam affected their thinking and sometimes their daily lives. Identify a similar far-reaching societal cause (for example, Columbine, drugs, rap music, blended families, AIDS and other STDs) and ask students to explain how that cause (or several of these causes) may have affected the experiences of their generation. How closely do they identify with each other, and how close in age of prior experience do their peers have to be in order to be part of their group, rather than part of an older generation out of synch with their own?

The Developing College Student
Virginia N. Gordon

This reading briefly summarizes the student development theories of two psychologists who have studied how college students develop in the cognitive, personal and social arenas. Most students can identify with many of the descriptions of thinking and behavior that the two theorists describe. Leading a discussion on their personal reactions to the stages outlined by both Perry and Chickering may help students gain insight into why and how they experience change in themselves and observe it in their peers. They may find some consolation in knowing that the "forces of growth" will persist and that certain thoughts and behaviors are a normal part of moving into adulthood.

Discussion Questions

1.   What aspect of student development does Perry's scheme address? What is its primary thesis?

      Perry theorizes how students grow and change intellectually and ethically. He describes the development of the thinking and reasoning processes that take place naturally as students proceed through their college years.

2.   How does the dualistic student view the world?

      Dualistic students view the world in polar terms. What they learn is either right or wrong, black or white. They like simplistic answers that emanate from an authority who is an expert with all the right answers. They also depend on these and other "experts" to make all their decisions for them. Can students identify with this dualistic stance? What specific instances can they remember when they felt this way?

3.   How does Perry describe "commitment," which is the most advanced phase of cognitive development?

      When students reach commitment, they have finally identified the content and style of their personal identity. They also understand that change and growth are inevitable and healthy. They make a commitment to a career area and are able to identify a life style that is truly theirs. What do your students think will help them eventually reach this stage of commitment that Perry describes?

4.   What are the seven developmental tasks of college students as proposed by Chickering?

      The seven tasks that all students must accomplish during their college years are: achieving competence, managing emotions, moving through autonomy toward interdependence, developing mature interpersonal relationships, establishing identity, developing purpose, and developing integrity.

5.   What, says Chickering, is required to develop an identity? How are the last two tasks of developing purpose and integrity related to establishing an identity?

      Establishing an identity comes only after the first four vectors are accomplished: developing competence, managing emotions, developing autonomy, and developing mature interpersonal relationships. Many students achieve this sense of identity during their sophomore or junior years. Developing purpose or a vocational sense of self becomes part of one's identity. Students' ability to clarify a personally valid set of values and beliefs is also important to identity formation, since standards for personal action and behavior are now set and act as guides for all behavior.

Suggested Activities

1. Put students into groups; ask them to discuss the "developing purpose" vector. How does Chickering's developmental task of--first, generally, and then specifically--selecting a career area run counter to most colleges' demand that students decide on an area of study immediately upon entering college? Would the students change this demand? If so how?

2. Ask someone in your counseling center or office of student affairs to give and interpret to your students the Student Developmental Task and Lifestyle Inventory. This self-scoring inventory is based on Chickering's vectors and provides information to the students on student activities, feelings, attitudes, aspirations, and relationships (e.g., educational involvement, career and lifestyle planning). The inventory takes about 30 minutes to complete. It is published by Student Development Associates, Inc., 110 Crestwood Drive, Athens, Georgia 3060.

The Thread
Denise Levertov

Gordon describes some of the thinking that psychologists have done about developmental tasks that college students face. The purpose of many of developmental tasks is to bring the individual to a sense of, and a comfort with, his or her identity. "The Thread" is also about identity, but the method of reaching self-knowledge is different for Levertov than for Perry or Chickering. Rather than survey many individuals about how they have developed, as psychologists often do, the poet Levertov examines her own memories and feelings. While she carries on her daily life, she says that she feels something gently and silently pulling at her, not from outside but from within. This feeling of who she is persists through her activities, sometimes surfacing, sometimes hiding away. When she thinks she has lost track of herself, she is sometimes surprised to find that this "something" that tugs at her is still there.

Discussion Questions

1. What is the "something" that Levertov describes? How do you know?

   We have suggested that the something is her sense of identity, of who she is. But students may have some alternative explanation. The challenge is to test any other explanation against the details of the poem to see if the alternative answers as many questions as "identity" seems to.

2. When Levertov says, "No barbed hook pierced or tore me," she seems to be comparing herself to a fish. Is she? If so, how does this influence your understanding of what's going on in this poem? If not, then why does she introduce barbed hooks that pierce and tear?

   In this part of the poem, the comparison to a fish on a hook and line is used for contrast: "NO barbed hook . . . ." Levertov is saying that the "something" that she feels is inside her, and while it may not be entirely within her control, it is not an external force, like the fisherman's hook and line.

3. Was she born with the "something" all her life, like a knot or a bridle?

   Levertov puts this as a question because she is not sure how the "something" developed. Was her sense of identity something she inherited from her parents, with her genes? Or did it develop out of very early experiences ("way back")? These are alternatives that she does not select from, though she is clear to say that the force is internal, not external ("No barbed hook . . .").

4. If Levertov has been living with this "something" all her life, why does it surprise her from time to time? How can that happen?

   She takes this "something" for granted sometimes, and at other times it is just "something" she has grown accustomed to. Then, once she has gotten used to it and no longer notices it, suddenly she steps a little out of bounds (beyond the limits that her own identity has set) and then she feels it again. And the self-knowledge of its persistence gives her a "stirring of wonder" and makes her catch her breath.

5. Is the "something" of the poem good or bad—or are those relevant words to describe it?

   Levertov does not seem upset by the knowledge that her identity controls or limits her, but some students may take a different point of view about their own reaction to their own feelings of identity. The poem gives no evidence that "the thread" is bad or good. Students making the judgment should have to show what <u>in the</u> <u>words of the poem</u> points them to such a conclusion either way.

Suggested Activities

1. Ask students to write down one or two events in their lives that have helped them to understand something important about themselves. Perhaps they found themselves in an unfamiliar environment and suddenly had to cope with out their usual support network of friends and family. (College can be such an environment, after all.) Have they learned any lessons about themselves from such an experience?

2. Achieving identity or a sense of self is one of the oldest and most pervasive themes in literature. Ask students if they have read any works that address this theme, then discuss some of them. Examples include *Huckleberry Finn*, *The Catcher in the Rye*, and more recently, the Star Wars movies.

Freshmen Can Be Taught to Think Creatively
Not Just Amass Information
David C. Finster

A previous reading by Virginia Gordon discusses William Perry's ideas on how college students develop cognitively and ethically. In this follow-up reading, Dr. Finster describes how he applies these ideas to his teaching of chemistry. Although he writes from a college teacher's perspective, discussion about this reading can center on the students' experiences with teachers who do not use developmental techniques versus those who do. Students can derive a better understanding of the dynamics of the classroom when they understand they are at one level cognitively and their instructors may be presenting material at another, usually higher cognitive level. How can students meet the challenge of this disparity?

Discussion Questions

1.   How has the work of Piaget, a French psychologist and philosopher, influenced Finster's understanding of cognition or how individuals learn in the broadest sense?

      It helped him understand how children learn to think about "problems and to make sense of the world around them." Piaget says we learn to think from a simplistic to a more complex and abstract way of thinking. Perry based much of his thinking on Piaget's work.

2.   Describe the dualists' way of thinking according to Perry.

      Dualists have a "right-or-wrong" view of the world. They like to memorize facts since these are the "right" answers given by an authority (the teacher).

3.   How can students be encouraged to progress beyond their current level of thinking?

      One way is for teachers to challenge students to think of the stage just beyond their current level and provide support as they do so.

4.   How does Finster describe a "good teacher"?

      A good teacher helps students think critically as they learn. Students need to learn how to evaluate different perspectives and challenge assumptions, which is the stage beyond the dualist's position.

5.   What specific steps does Finster take to apply Perry's ideas in his teaching chemistry?

      Finster uses a developmental instructional method. He recognizes where students are in their intellectual growth. He challenges the way students think by presenting alternative perspectives to scientific problems as often as possible. He focuses on the process of learning as much as the content of the course. How one solves a problem is as important as the solution itself. He also espouses small classes with a great deal of teacher-student interaction.

Suggested Activities

I.   Ask students to debate the pros and cons of teaching students in large classroom settings versus small classes. How do these two learning environments benefit or not benefit the students, the instructors, and the institution? Ask students to describe the ideal type of learning environment they prefer.

2.   If there is a faculty member on your campus who is knowledgeable about student development theory, ask her/him to lead a discussion in your class on Perry's or Chickering's ideas and how students can approach their academic work with this knowledge.

College Pressures
William Zinsser

Many students can certainly relate with Zinsser's description of students under pressure. Many freshmen, especially, will still want to please the significant other people in their lives, notably their parents. Almost every student feels some degree of academic pressure. By discussing these pressures, perhaps students can understand their own motivations and behavior. As Zinsser puts it, "Ultimately it will be the students' own business to break the circles in which they are trapped."

Discussion Questions

1. The author says there are four kinds of pressures working on college students today. What are they? Can you think of others?

   The four types of pressures are: economic, parental, peer, and self-induced. Older students may feel family and work pressures. Students newly out of high school may also feel social pressures.

2. What kind of pressures does the author indicate come from parents? What is the motivation for these pressures?

   Parents want a secure future for their children and want them to major in something practical, where there is a direct relationship to a promising career. Parents often encourage their children into professional fields for which they have no interest. Students can discuss the type of pressures they are feeling from their parents. Which of these are "self-induced"?

3. What other kinds of pressures do students feel? Give an example from the reading.

   Students also feel peer pressure and self-induced pressure, which are often "intertwined." An example from the reading describes students who do more than they are expected to, thus making it more difficult for students who do normal work. Grade fever is often the cause and effect for overachievers.

4. How do students react to these pressures?

   Some get sick; some are "blocked"; some sleep too little or oversleep. Some overexert. The students can describe other reactions they or their peers might have, depending on the pressure that is being exerted. Are students always aware of why they are reacting as they do?

5. How do these pressures affect the faculty and other professionals on campus?

   When teachers get increasing efforts from their classes, their expectations rise accordingly. The faculty are often not aware of the pressures that some students exert upon their peers when they submit work that far exceeds the assignment. The result of these pressures are often dealt with by deans and counselors. Have the students ever experienced a class where the competition obviously places pressure on them to produce above what is expected?

Suggested Activities

1. Invite a counselor from the campus counseling center to discuss stress management with your class.

2. Present a case study of a student who is experiencing a particular type of stress. Put students in small groups to discuss the case study and ask them to offer possible ways to alleviate the stress that results from the case study student's dilemma.

Dorm Do's and Don'ts
E. Gordon Gee

This brief essay is directed to those students who live in a residence hall. While Dr. Gee offers practical advice (e.g., don't put red sweatshirts and white socks in the same laundry load), he also encourages students to take advantage of the opportunity to learn about human relationships.

Discussion Questions

1.   What does the author suggest you can learn from dorm living?

      Students can increase their understanding of the world and how humans relate to each other; lasting friendships can be made; and they learn to be independent, learning from their mistakes. Commuter students can discuss what they are learning from their common experience and how they can learn to make friends and be independent in their situation.

2.   If you are experiencing dorm life, is your experience similar to that described by the author?

      A class discussion can encourage students to share their experiences living in a residence hall. Students who do not live in a residence hall can be asked to share a typical day for them as well.

3.   What other experiences or lessons have you learned from living in a residence hall?

      Students may want to debate the advantages and disadvantages of living in a residence hall. Commuter students may want equal time to offer their perspectives.

Suggested Activities:

1.   If you have residence halls on your campus, ask students to discuss the advantages and disadvantages living in a dorm vs. student apartment living. What are the advantages and disadvantages of living in a residence hall vs. being a commuter? Living in a fraternity or sorority house?

2.   If you don't have residence halls at your college, ask students to discuss how your campus would change if you did. How would the make-up of the student body change? Would there be any advantages for building a residence hall(s) on your campus?

Loneliness
Barbara M. Newman and Phillip R. Newman

Many students experience loneliness, especially in the first weeks of college. For some this is their first extended period away from family, friends and familiar environments. A few remain lonely throughout their college years. The uprootedness some students feel may be the result of a lack of experiences which could prepare them for more independent behavior. Students may be able to identify with the three types of loneliness outlined in the reading. Even students who commute daily from home may experience a sense of uprootedness when they begin college. By discussing this concern students may realize that they are not the only ones experiencing this feeling. Emphasizing ways to alleviate or at least soften the effects of loneliness can help students learn how to deal with it.

Discussion Questions

1. What factors may trigger loneliness in a college student?

    Leaving the familiarity of family, friends and places can trigger feelings of loneliness as students enter a new and sometimes foreign college environment. Breaking ties with old friends can also bring feelings of loss. Can the students describe any other factors that trigger loneliness for them?

2. What are the three categories of loneliness described by the authors?

    The three categories are transient (lasting a short time and passing); situational (brought on by a sudden loss or move to a new environment); and chronic (long-term). Ask students to give an example for each category.

3. How does transient loneliness differ from chronic loneliness?

    Transient loneliness is of short duration and occurs when a person is alone for a brief period of time. Chronic loneliness lasts a long time and may be the direct result of a specific event or situation. Students who experience chronic loneliness often are lacking in social skills; for them, making meaningful contacts with others is difficult.

4. Why are students with little or no social support more vulnerable to illness?

    When students find it difficult to replace the "level of trust and closeness" they experienced at home, they are more vulnerable to chronic loneliness and illness.

5. How do friendships help students feel less lonely?

    Developing new friendships is a key to adjusting to the new college environment. Friends can support you by including you in social and other activities. They can be sensitive to moods of "preoccupation and discouragement" that lead to loneliness. They can offer the type of relationship and support that many students need as they begin to adjust to a new environment. Students can share their experiences with making friends and how this has helped them adjust to college life.

Suggested Activities

1. Put students into pairs and ask them to share with their partner any feelings of loneliness they have or are experiencing as a result of being in college. Suggest to them they discuss ways of overcoming these feelings.

2. Ask the class to discuss the elements of friendship and how its importance can affect people's lives. What are the characteristics of a "good friend"? How do new friends become "old" friends?

3. Invite a counselor from your Counseling Center to speak to the class about adjustment concerns that are common among new students, including loneliness which might lead to depression and other problems.

UNIT 3

HOW CAN I SUCCEED ACADEMICALLY?

Even though first year students usually have the skills to perform adequately, they often come to college with a poor understanding of their ability to succeed academically. This unit will augment their understanding about skills and abilities essential to college work and success in the world thereafter. Through these readings students can gain some wisdom and perspective on the outcomes they should strive for in college. Instructors may wish to add class discussion of study skills, test-taking, and time management.

UNIT 3 READINGS

What Students Must Know to Succeed in the 21st Century
Donna Uchida

Donna Uchida summarizes the thinking of carefully selected educators, business leaders, and government officials who served as an advisory board of 55 advisers. They identified skills that they think will be needed to succeed in the new century. Commentary includes some suggestions on how to develop those skills and some analysis of how they will be useful.

Discussion Questions

1. What is the purpose behind Uchida's frequent quotations from members of the Council of 55?

    Uchida is presenting this set of results not as her own original thinking but as the result of discussions with many other people—in fact, 55 of them. She introduces the many citations for several reasons: 1) to give credit where it is due, to the person(s) who suggested the idea; 2) to provide specific authority for each section, and she hopes (we suspect) that readers will see the wide range of points of view that have come to a generally consistent way of advising students to prepare for success in life after college; 3) to add interest to what is essentially a list by using specific examples to enliven the writing. Are there other reasons the class can think of?

2. Are there any kinds of knowledge that surprised you by being included on this list? Are there any omissions that you can think of?

    Some of our colleagues were surprised at the inclusion of "an understanding of issues surrounding patriotism." While many agreed with this inclusion, they were surprised to find someone willing to speak out about it. Our students seemed most surprised by the inclusion of geography as a subject to study for success in the future. However, some reflection on the question (see Uchida's analysis) leads to the conclusion that it is very difficult to understand events in a complex world without some sense of where they are occurring and therefore how they may affect places both near them and far away.

3. How would you rank these the kinds of knowledge from most important to least important? If you need to put some of them together into categories, feel free to do so, but explain why you think they fit together.

A useful way to approach this question with students is to decide <u>on what basis</u> these skills should be ranked. Students may get different rankings by using different criteria: for example, rank these according to usefulness in a career and you'll come up with one ordering, but rank them according to personal satisfaction in later life and you may get a very different ordering.

4. Uchida lists the ability to get along with others (item 2) as an "academic content" area. Is it? Why or why not?

Business leaders report more and more frequently that recent graduates have not had the ability to work on teams. As a result, our own department of mathematics has been asked to teach the calculus sequence required of business students using a small group approach. That way, it is hoped, students will get familiar with small group dynamics and realize that sometimes they are judged by how they can work effectively toward a group goal.

The above paragraph may not answer Uchida's question, but it provides a context from which to consider it. Similar efforts toward group participation have been used in Communications classes for a long while, and it can be argued that any Journalism program that includes a student newspaper as part of the graded outcome is also an academic setting that teaches teamwork. Are there others?

Suggested Activity

Invite students to set up their own equivalent to Uchida's Council of 55. For example, you might ask the members of one third of a class each to interview another student about what will be needed for success in the 21st century. A second third could then interview other faculty members, and the remainder might be encouraged to talk with businessmen or other professionals. (The group that has to talk with instructors will be gaining an important experience that new students often report as a source of anxiety: meeting with faculty members outside of class! You will be doing them a service to help them learn to start a conversation with a teacher.) Then have them come back together to critique Uchida's list from the perspectives that they have gained.

Major Decisions
James Tunstead Burtchaell

Father Burtchaell explores the reasons that Notre Dame allows freshmen to declare an "intention" but not a major field of study. He mentions the fact that as we grow, we change, and that students starting college are entering one of the greatest periods of growth in their lives--so changes should be expected. Maturity brings with it a sense of perspective and an understanding that "any major can lead to any career, and that the best major is the one you choose with no lookout out of the corner of your eye to where it will lead." Quoting nineteenth-century English educator William Johnson Cory, Burtchaell points out that "above all, you go to a great school for self-knowledge." Surprisingly for many, he urges students to select as their major field that area of study which they enjoy most.

Discussion Questions

1. What are the three difficulties that cause undergraduates to make wrong initial decisions about a major?

    The subjects are unknown (that is, as freshmen students have only their previous high school courses to as a basis for judgment); the choice is so pressured, by parents, high school guidance counselors, and others; and the competition is so strong. Do you students agree that these are the major difficulties that stand in the way of their making a good initial decision about a major? Are there others?

2. For Burtchaell, what distinguishes training from education? Give some examples of your own for training.

    Burtchaell writes: "An institution that offers you training is trying to provide you with the information and skills you need for a specific career." Education, on the other hand, "is the opportunity, through studying a variety of subjects, to gain the information and the dexterity to use your wits and your expression. Education prepares you to *be* someone more than to do something." His examples of training include law school, a welding academy, and advanced training in computing. Other examples could include courses of study in engineering, business, teaching kindergarten through 12th grade, architecture, pharmacy, chiropractic, nursing, automobile repair, real estate and insurance sales--to name a few examples that students may suggest. Most European universities still preserve the distinction between training and education that Burtchaell describes.

3. What should a "good university" provide its students according to Burtchaell?

    A "good university," says Burtchaell, "will give you quite a few skills and a broad grounding of information" but will in addition develop students "whose mind is enlivened and whose imagination is limber." Ask students what they think Burtchaell means by an enlivened mind and a limber imagination. Are these attributes important to them? Why, or why not?

4. Based on your experience and that of your friends, is Burtchaell correct in saying that freshmen have insufficient information to select a major?

    You may wish to ask students to identify what kind, and how much, information they ought to have in order to make a sound decision about a major. What would they need to know in order to make a good decision about buying a used car, or deciding on a foreign country to visit? How would they go about getting that information? What lessons does the general process for making a good decision teach them when the question is, what should I select as my major?

5.   Burtchaell's final two sentences may have surprised you. Did you expect a serious teacher to draw this conclusion? How does he justify it?

        Burtchaell closes his essay as follows: "Your duty is to enjoy. Nothing you might do could be more useful." We rarely think of a "duty" as something we will enjoy. Why does Burtchaell combine these two notions in his conclusion? What might students think would be a better standard of judgment than "enjoyment"? Compare their alternatives with Burtchaell's assertion.

Suggested Activities

1.   Invite students to keep a list or a diary of the things about college that surprise them. What academic differences from high school do they discover? Are subjects that they used to enjoy becoming tiresome or worse? Have they discovered any new areas they had not expected to like?

2.   Suggest that students imagine themselves suddenly in possession of great wealth. Suppose, for example, that they have won a lottery that will pay a million dollars annually for the rest of their lives. For most of them, travel, partying, and other means of relaxation will become boring in a year or so, and education will be attractive not as a way to earn a living but rather as a way to learn to live. Have each student list 15 or 20 classes that he or she would take purely for interest, not for any kind of payoff. What do they learn?

College Major Doesn't Mean All That Much
William Raspberry

Raspberry's advice to his daughter as she enters college is very similar to Burtchaell's--and indeed, Raspberry quotes Burtchaell in his own brief column. He endorses three principles for students to remember: (1) aside from vocational fields like (he says) engineering or computer science, "any relationship between majors and careers is largely incidental"; (2) students and colleges should delay the necessity of choosing a major for as long as practicable; and (3) pick your major based on what you enjoy (following Burtchaell). He encourages students to develop a liberal arts foundation to which they add career related experience and personal initiative.

Discussion Questions

1.   What reasons does William Raspberry give for his assertion that your choice of a major is not as important as many college students think?

      He draws from his own experience, in which none of his four different college majors related to his own eventual career in journalism. He also relates the advice of others, like John Willson, history professor at Michigan's Hillsdale College. Ask your students how important the choice of a major is to them. Have any already changed their direction since, say, the plans they made a year ago?

2.   How do you react to Raspberry's thesis that any relationship between majors and careers is "largely incidental"? Why is this perceived connection made by so many students?

      Raspberry is trying to ease his daughter's "frenzy" about making a decision. The same panic and fear of not having a solid niche to call their own are feelings that many students suffer. "Relax," Raspberry advises them all, because except for vocational areas, the tie between careers and major is at best unpredictable. Let your students tell you why they connect major and career so tightly. Are they afraid to undertake a career for which they have not been trained by their educators? Raspberry's view implies that they will need to rely more on themselves as educated persons than on their training.

Suggested Activities

1.   Invite an academic adviser who is a generalist to your class to provide an overview of the academic majors offered by your institution. Ask the adviser to include an explanation of how the "liberal arts" or general education courses required in your curriculum build the foundation for the baccalaureate or associate's degree.

2.   Arrange a panel of alumni from various occupations to discuss in class how their "major" relates to the job they are actually doing today; what courses benefited them the most? What courses do they wish they had taken while in college?

Fourteen Ways of Looking at Electives
Thomas L. Minnick

Minnick's essay is explicitly about how to make good use of electives, but it also applies more generally to the kinds of factors students should have in mind whenever they make choices about what to take--when they schedule for next term, or when they consider their curriculum choices overall. One goal of the essay is to show readers that where they have options in course selections, their decisions can reflect a variety of purposes and values. Choice 14--take courses that you enjoy--repeats a theme found throughout the essays in this unit.

Discussion Questions

1. How are electives defined in this reading? How do they fit into the general structure of degree requirements?

    Electives are defined as those courses which are not prescribed as requirements. They are "what is left over"--the difference between courses that explicitly designated as requirements and the minimum credit total required for completion of the degree. Since the number of electives possible in a degree depends on the program and the specific institution, instructors can use the first paragraphs of this essay as a time to identify and review (1) the courses required by all undergraduate degrees at the institution, (2) the courses required by all degrees within a category of programs (e.g., the requirements for a liberal arts degree, or for a B.S. in Business Administration, or for a B.S. in Education), and (3) the courses required for a specific program (e.g., the requirements for a History major or for a program in Physical Therapy).

2. What kind of electives can enhance your chances of finding a satisfying career?

    Most two- and four-year colleges now offer introductory courses in career decision-making. These classes usually focus on two subjects: (1) the talents, training, and interests of the individual who is seeking a career direction, and (2) the world of available work as defined by several authoritative surveys of occupations. Taken seriously, these courses can help a student lay the groundwork for a satisfying career choice. In addition, classes that teach specific business-related skills (accounting, marketing, advertising, personal finance) can enhance any student's preparation to serve in a business role.

3. Through what kind of electives can you acquire skills and knowledge that may be useful for your future leisure time activities?

    Courses in health and physical education, in music and art, and in any area of a strong avocational interest can answer the need identified in this question. An effective way to enlarge the list is to ask students first, what are their interests, apart from their intended major program?, and then, what courses offered at your institution can help to educate the students in more depth about those interests? Another effective answer is to point to course that incorporate volunteer work (such a tutoring others) in the syllabus of activities.

4. Although taking extra courses in your major is not listed as a way to use elective hours, would this use of course be a way to increase your mastery of the subject? Why or why not is this a good idea?

    It seems reasonable to suppose that additional training in the major will help students increase their mastery of that subject. However, most institutions place a limit on the number of courses or credits a student can earn in the field of the major. Additionally, students should ask whether their interest in achieving greater mastery might be better served by taking an advanced degree (a Master's, for example) in the major area. Most students will be better served in the long by avoiding too great an emphasis on a single field in the undergraduate program.

At least, that is our thinking about the matter. Ask students what they think, and play the Devil's Advocate if you don't find a variety of opinions among the students in your class.

5. How can you expand your understanding and appreciation of other cultures through electives? Why is this a particularly good use of electives today?

Students should remember that requirements are always stated as the least they need to do to earn a degree. Even if your institution does not require cross-cultural education (through courses in the history, art, or culture of another nation, or through foreign language study), students preparing to live most of their lives in the 21st century would be wise to anticipate the challenges of that century as far as we can predict them. By all projections, by very early in the 21st century the United States will have no majority culture. Classes in geography, cultural anthropology, sociology of various cultural groups--these and many other courses that focus on how to understand and value our differences will help prepare students for the future.

Suggested Activities

1. Divide your class into four or five small groups, and assign each group two or three of the fourteen uses Minnick identifies for electives. Ask the members of each group to list and report on four or five courses at your institution that would be included in each of their categories.

2. Minnick's title is roughly borrowed from a poem by Wallace Stevens called "Sixteen Ways of Looking at a Blackbird." Help Minnick catch up to Stevens by asking students to identify two more uses of electives that do not overlap with the fourteen in the essay.

The Right Stuff: Research Strategies for the Internet Age
Nancy O'Hanlon

One skill that students need for success after college is the ability to find accurate, up-to-date authoritative information. As the amount of information available to us multiplies, the ability to do effective research becomes increasingly important. The Internet provides access to masses of information, but researchers need to be able to locate what they need and evaluate what they find on the World Wide Web. Moreover, the ease of access to Web-based information should not cause students to forget about books and periodicals, the traditional and continuing location of much that they may need to know.

Discussion Questions

1. What is the difference between a Web index and a Web directory?

A Web directory is a list of websites that someone or some group has compiled for users. It is an existing data base to which you might go as you would to a printed bibliography, which is also a list, usually of books or articles on a specific subject. Sometimes a Web directory is annotated with information about each website, just as some bibliographies include the author's description and review of each source.

A Web index is a search engine—a program that searches the Web for you when you ask for information on a topic. (Our current favorite is Google, but others include Yahoo, Alta-vista, and Infoseek.) Because of the capabilities of the Internet and of these programs, they work on demand: when you type in a term and press enter, the Web index searches out and lists websites that match your inquiry.

2. What does O'Hanlon mean when she talks about a "search strategy"?

Trained as a research librarian, O'Hanlon knows that unskilled researchers waste a lot of time when they don't have a plan for their research work. A good search strategy starts with general resources (like encyclopedias and subject dictionaries) and proceeds to more specific sources from there. Whether these sources are Web-based or printed materials or both, researchers can be more effective and efficient by starting with a plan.

3. Explain the use of these signs in searching for information on the Web: +, -, and " ".

These signs are called search qualifiers. The plus (+) sign between terms that you are searching tells your search engine that you are interested in sources that have all the terms connected by this qualifier. Otherwise, some search engines will list sources that have only one of the terms you're looking for: with the + sign, you'll get a much shorter list that is less likely to include materials you don't want. The minus (-) sign tells the search engine to omit results with the term preceded by the –. Quotation marks signify that the words within them should be treated as a phrase.

4. What kind of questions should you ask when evaluating a website? Give some examples that O'Hanlon does not provide for evaluating a website with respect to its purpose, authority, and content.

Effective researchers are critical thinkers about the materials they find. The old warning, "Don't believe everything you read in the papers" applies many times over to items you find on the Internet. To publish something on the Web requires virtually no expertise, and search engines do not evaluate the sites they locate—they just present them to you.

So get into the habit of asking critical questions about each website you use. How old is the information it presents? How often is it updated? Who wrote it? Do the authors have credentials related to the subject of the site? How extensive is the information? What kind of sources do the authors cite? Why did they put together the information that they provide? Many websites are commercial: if an automobile company authored the site you're looking at, don't expect negative reviews of their product to be there!

These and other questions can be summarized as related to the purpose, authority, and content of the site—as O'Hanlon tells us.

5. O'Hanlon says that we still need to consult books for much of our information. Is she right? Explain your answer.

This is a good question to let students talk about, but you'll need to get them talking. Seed questions might be: What have you recently had to look up on the Web? Could you have found that information somewhere else? How would you go about learning the official rules that govern World Cup Soccer play? Where would you find for the complete works of a nineteenth century female poet? How can you locate historical and current information about earthquakes in Latin America? Select topics of relevance to the course or to specific assignments and students will pay close attention if they are wise.

Suggested Activities

1. Make a list of subjects that students might find interesting. Use brief entries, such as KISS, FBI, Amazon rain forest, HIV, euros, tall ships, and the like. Require students to identify one printed source and one web-based source for information about each of the items.

2. Chances are very good that your college or university library is larger than any your students have previously confronted. Invite a librarian to come to class and talk with them about how to be effective researchers in your campus library.

Please! It's Only Seven Minutes Late, Professor
Joel J. Gold

This light essay describes one professor's experience with a situation that is familiar to many students: What happens when they turn in late papers? Discussion can center around their own experiences with this particular dilemma and how different instructors react to assignments being turned in late.

Discussion Questions

1.   What happened to the student who turned in her paper seven minutes late?

     She was surprised to find her paper being tugged at under the door and then heard it being torn into bits. She also heard the professor enjoying his little game.

2.   How did Gold get even with the class that began to doubt his story about the paper shredder? What was their reaction?

     He pretended in class that the six late papers had been put into the paper shredder. As he was dumping the supposedly shredded themes on the desk, students exploded with laughter and general pandemonium.

3.   How did one class "get even" with the author? How did Gold react to their prank?

     His honors satire class handed in their papers in a shredded condition, although the real papers had been given to the office secretaries. Although he doesn't say specifically, Gold enjoyed their prank and knew he had finally met his match.

Suggested Activities

1.   Ask students to discuss two points of view about late papers: from the professor's perspective and from the students' perspective. Should late papers be penalized? How might an employer react to an employee turning in late assignments?

2.   Ask students to list the actions they might take in order to eliminate turning in late assignments (e.g., early research on the topic, detailed note taking, outlining first).

Why I Don't Let Students Cut My Classes
William R. Brown

This essay offers students an opportunity to see a professor's reaction to a common occurrence--that of cutting classes. It can open a discussion on why students cut classes and their perspectives on the consequences of their actions. Although some instructors do not take attendance or seem to "care" about students not showing up, this reading can offer insights into how much care and thought most teachers give to the preparation and presentation of their classes. It can also challenge student attitudes and behaviors about the classroom experience.

Discussion Questions

1. What, according to Brown, does research indicate about academic success as related to class attendance?

    Brown cites some recent research that indicates attending classes is more important to academic success than other factors, such as the amount of time spent studying. He also offers his own feelings about students who do not attend his class after he has spent so much time in preparation. This last point might not have occurred to some students.

2. What happened after the author instituted his no-cut rule?

    Student performance "improved markedly," especially in the bottom rank of students. Students might be asked for their opinions on why this happened, especially to the bottom rank.

3. What benefits did he see after enforcing the policy?

    Both student and teacher morale were higher. Discussions were better and assignments were generally turned in on time. Who were the real beneficiaries of his policy?

4. What reaction did he get from his colleagues?

    He did not receive much support from his colleagues. They seemed to accept that a certain percentage of students were not going to show up for their class. Some felt students were responsible for their own learning and that they (the teachers) were not "liable for their losses." Students might discuss what is lost when students cut classes. Is it the teacher's or students' responsibility for making sure classes are not cut except for valid reasons? Why should they attend when the professor is "boring"? How can they still benefit from attending such a class?

5. Why, according to Brown, do students cut classes?

    Brown says they "cut because they are allowed to." Students are given the impression that they are free to cut even though they are hurting themselves. They also cut because they are not prepared for class or are feeling inadequate. Brown makes some excellent points from a teacher's perspective. Why do students think they and other students cut classes? What are some positive steps to prevent this? Would they appreciate a "no-cut" policy for their classes? Would the decision then be taken out of their hands? What would be some consequences for them personally?

Suggested Activities

1.   Ask students to list on the board their reasons for cutting class. Ask them to separate the valid reasons from the non-valid ones.

2.   Ask students to write a brief essay on why or why not there should be a "no-cut" policy at your institution.

HOW SHOULD I EXPECT TO LEARN?

This unit was added to this second edition because learning is such an integral part of a student's reason for being in college and new research on this subject has prompted insights into the learning process. There is increased interest now in service and distance learning, two areas that were used by only small groups of students in the past. Helping students understand how they personally approach learning as well as appreciating its complexities will hopefully influence how they actually practice it.

The readings in this unit represent a variety of approaches to the subject. Siebert and Gilpin and Twining present more useable ideas about learning, while James adds a more theoretical perspective. Waterman's essay on service learning defines an approach to learning that, although not new, is increasingly being implemented on more campuses. If you have service learning in any form on your campus, this reading will provide an historical and general description of it's intent. Governati, Steele, and Carey and the Illinois Online Network offer background information on another approach to learning that many students need to appreciate. Although some adult students may have a keener interest in distance learning than traditional-age students at present, both need to understand how it might have an impact on their future education.

UNIT 4 READINGS

Understanding Who Is Smart
Jennifer James

Jennifer James offers a broader perspective on the definition of intelligence than many students recognize. She challenges students to think about their own strengths and weaknesses in this area. She also describes different styles or ways that people think. She encourages students to consider how they apply their personal style to different types of problem-solving situations. James suggests that as our understanding of intelligence evolves, more complex patterns of thought are developing. She projects that in the future students will be required to think in more fluid ways, so how they learn to adapt their patterns of "reacting and responding" will determine how their basic intelligence develops. Students should take to heart many of the ideas that James presents so they will be able to examine how they approach the learning process, and how they can acquire or improve those aspects of learning that are important in their role of college student.

Discussion Questions

1. In her first paragraph, Jennifer James provides her own definition of intelligence. What is it?

   She is arguing for a broad-based definition of intelligence that includes a way to predict "real world success." She suggests that intelligence is the ability to react to new and old situations by the way one thinks and acts. Instead of memorizing facts and figures, the current emphasis is on building "thinking skills" that force one to engage in a more complicated series of thought processes.

2. What traits seem to be important in Nelson Goodman's expanded concept of intelligence?

   Goodman changed the question from "How smart is he?" to "*How* is she smart?" Although motivation and interest are important, other traits are just as influential. These include concentration, intention, purpose, drive and tenacity.

3. Why are Howard Gardner's eight basic forms of intelligence important in broadening our concept of intelligence? Is the form that James adds to Gardner's list different from the others? How?

Gardner doesn't agree with the traditional, one-dimensional view of intelligence, but presents a multifaceted approach that takes into account how an individual "solves problems and fashions products." He points out people have different cognitive strengths and cognitive styles, as well as different combinations of intelligence. By broadening this concept of intelligence, Gardner expands our understanding of how and why individuals are so different from one another. James points out, for example, that the highest order of thinking and reasoning is found in intrapersonal intelligence. New research is showing how music can affect the neural networks of the brain in individuals who are using their talents in this area. Identifying these different forms of intelligences has great implications for teaching and learning.

James adds "practical intelligence" to Gardner's list. She describes this as common sense or the ability to unconsciously solve everyday problems. James argues that this form is different from the other intelligences because it is not consciously implemented. It is difficult if not impossible to measure common sense because it is done subconsciously.

4. Do you agree with the author's addition of "practical intelligence"? Why?

Common sense has long been recognized as sound judgment when applied to solving daily life problems. It could also be described as an unreflective opinion. Whether this is a form of intelligence depends on how you define it. If we return to Gardner's definition, that is, how an individual solves problems and fashions products, then one could argue that it is a form of intelligence. One could also argue that it is a combination of some of the other intelligences included in Gardner's list and does not stand alone.

5. What is "lateral thinking"? How can it be used in problem solving?

Lateral thinking is sometimes called "critical thinking" or "system thinking." It uses a broad set of thinking ools that includes combining disparate parts into a coherent whole. It involves viewing a problem from all sides and identifying all alternatives before devising a solution. This is particularly useful for group problem solving, since it can help the group focus on the task, and allows group members to discuss their reactions and responses while looking for common ground.

6. What are the characteristics of "system thinking" according to the author? How can system thinking be used to analyze problem areas?

Like lateral thinking, system thinking is viewing the whole to understand its parts. Rather than looking at its component parts in isolation when trying to solve a problem, examining it in context or its entirety can help us understand how all the parts are connected; when one part is challenged, the rest are affected. System thinking can help us view the big picture, and helps us examine the inter-relatedness of all the parts. In this way, we can uncover the real causes that, as the author suggests, may be hidden in the system.

Suggested Activities

1. Ask students to complete the rating sheet of intelligences on page 109. Discuss the question posed in the exercise.

2. Present the following idea (or make up one of your own): "All students should be able to get a college degree free of cost." Place students in small groups and instruct them to use PMI (Plus, Minus, Interesting) to evaluate the idea. Discuss the results in the context of lateral or system thinking.

Learning Styles: They Can Help or Hinder
Al Siebert and Bernadine Gilpin

This essay may help students understand why they perform in some classes and with some teachers better than others. It will also provide insights into how they learn best based on their own temperament. Siebert and Gilpin not only describe different styles of learning but also offer some practical tips for applying these approaches to a classroom setting.

Discussion Questions

1. What is a learning style?

    It is the unique approach or method that individuals employ in the process of learning. Some studies have shown that identifying a student's style and then providing instruction congruent with that style can lead to more effective learning.

2. What is the difference between the auditory and visual style of learning?

    Auditory learners learn best by listening. They are more apt to retain information when they can hear it first. Visual learners learn best by reading the information. If they can see it in print, they are more apt to retain it.

3. How does temperament affect your approaches to learning?

    Temperament refers to a person's natural disposition. Individuals will characteristically react to certain situations in a predictable manner. One's temperament will influence how a person will approach a specific learning situation.

4. What aspects of learning does the left brain control? What aspects does the right brain control?

    The "thinking versus feeling" dimension of temperament that the Myers-Briggs Type Indicator (MBTI) measures is closely associated with left brain/right-brain research. The left brain is associated with remembering words, using logic, and thinking analytically. The left-brain "thinks in a linear fashion" and is "time-oriented." The right-brain is associated with visual, emotional, irrational thinking and emotional logic. It is the source of creativity and intuition." Right-brain thinking allows you to visualize and think in patterns that jump from one spot to another without apparent logic or reason. As an instructor, if you have an interest in this area, you might want to obtain a copy of *Success, Your Style!* by Matte and Henderson which is listed in the Unit 3 Summary.

5. What four temperaments can influence your learning style? Describe them and how they affect the way you learn.

    The four temperaments that the Myers-Briggs Type Indicator (MBTI) measures are: Extroversion versus Introversion, Thinking versus Feeling, Sensation versus Intuition, and Judging versus Perceiving. Students can discuss how these four dimensions influence the way they think, communicate, and learn, based on the descriptions in the reading. If you have an interest in this area, you might want to enlarge on the descriptions from other material that is available from many sources, such as the *MBTI Manual, Gifts Differing* by Isabel Briggs Myers (Consulting Psychologists Press, 1980), *People Types and Tiger Stripes* by

Gordon Lawrence (Center for Applications for Psychological Type, Inc., 1979), or *Please Understand Me* by David Keirsey and Marilyn Bates (Prometheus Nemesis Books, 1978).

Suggested Activity

Ask a Myers-Briggs Type Indicator expert from your Counseling Center, Psychology Department, or Education department to give and interpret the MBTI to the students in your class. The interpretation can include how students learn according to the dimensions offered in the instrument. The Keirsey Temperament Sorter may also be used for this purpose (in *Please Understand Me* by Keirsey and Bates listed above). An instrument that focuses entirely on learning styles is the *Learning Style Inventory* by David A. Kolb (McBer and Company, 1985).

Active Learning
James Twining

This essay emphasizes that successful learners are the students who take charge of, or responsibility for their own learning. This essay is perhaps the most practical reading in this unit since it describes different techniques that can lead to becoming an active learner. Twining discusses three critical stages in the learning process and although he includes some common study techniques such as note taking and self-testing, he provides a logical organization for controlling how one approaches the learning process.

Discussion Questions

1. What do some research studies indicate about successful learners, as cited by the author?

   Students who use good study techniques such as underlining key ideas and taking notes remember more of what they study than those who do not. Those who are actively involved in improving their study methods are more likely to be successful learners. Students who are aware and actively think about *how* they are learning will become even more adept.

2. What does Twining mean by "learning to learn"?

   Learning to learn means understanding how one learns best and the type of strategies that work most effectively, including the routine use of good study habits. When all facets of "learning to learn" are in place, chances of becoming a successful learner are enhanced.

3. What are the four types of information you must have to formulate a plan for learning, according to the author?

   The four types of information that are essential for planning are: the characteristics of the learner, the critical tasks or specific assignments, the nature of the materials, and the learning strategies necessary to complete the task. These are summarized in Figure 1.

4. What three basic strategies does Twining suggest for monitoring your comprehension in reading?

   Twining suggests three basic strategies for monitoring reading comprehension: note taking, questioning, and summarizing. Note-taking forces you think about what you are reading and increases your ability to understand and remember the most important points. Questioning helps to identify important ideas and to think of possible answers. Summarizing helps identify key elements and helps organize large amounts of information into a condensed, more easily remembered version.

5. How can you evaluate whether your learning is successful?

    Self-testing can help you evaluate your understanding of the subject before the actual test. Reviewing the material before a test can also determine if you have retained the information. The author offers a few basic strategies to increase memory during the review process. They are spaced study, active rehearsal or recitation, overlearning, and relearning.

Suggested Activities

1. Invite a professional from your campus learning skills center to discuss basic study skills that may lead to becoming a successful, active learner.

2. Invite a faculty member from the psychology or education department to class who is an expert on learning. Ask him or her to discuss learning styles and how an understanding of one's personal approach to learning can be beneficial. (If possible, ask her or him to give a learning-styles inventory so students can apply this information personally.)

An Overview of Service Learning
Alan Waterman

Service-learning has seen renewed interest on college campuses in the last decade. As Waterman points out, service-learning was a part of our society long before it was considered a form of "experiential learning." He provides a formal definition for this approach to education. As they experience service to the community, students not only learn through active participation, but they also have the opportunity to reflect on it as they think, talk, and write about it in the classroom. Waterman also makes the distinction between service-learning and volunteer service. Service-learning provides a opportunity for students to relate subject matter to their lives outside of the classroom and can help them apply the knowledge and skills taught in the classroom. Waterman points out the value of service-learning in career exploration and in developing self-efficacy and self-esteem, not to mention the real service it provides to the community.

Discussion Questions

1. What is service learning? How is it different from volunteer service?

   It is an educational method that involves students in active participation in a community that is integrated into students' academic curriculum. Service-learning extends learning beyond the classroom into community activity. Through real-life situations students can acquire and use skills and knowledge that are not only educational, but foster the development of a sense of caring for others. In volunteer service no opportunity is provided to formally relate service activities to the educational value of the experience.

2. Identify some of the historical roots of service learning.

   In service-learning the American tradition of service to the community is joined with the value of experiential learning. Waterman reminds us that the value of service to the community is reflected in the writings of Thomas Jefferson and William James. The United States government has created community service projects in the past and present.

   The Civilian Conservation Corps (CCC) program during the Great Depression is an example of how millions of youth were able to provide service to the environment and society. John F. Kennedy created the Peace Corps through which thousands of individuals still provide many types of service worldwide. John Dewey, the noted philosopher and educator, long ago espoused the notion that experiential learning not only helps students apply what they learn, but provides an opportunity to perform service to the greater community.

3. How, according to Waterman, can service-learning lead to better career choices?

Many students make career decisions based on very little real-life knowledge or experience in the areas they are considering. Through service-learning, students can be exposed to a wide variety of work environments that may not only help them confirm or disconfirm a choice, but could open up new possibilities that were not previously considered.

4. Waterman argues that service-learning can teach civic responsibility. Do you agree?

    This will depend on how individual students perceive the learning situation in which they are involved. If, for example, they are experiencing a service-learning project that involves the environment, they may become more reflective about issues pertaining to government's role in this area. Waterman is careful to point out that from an educational perspective, the goal is to promote the *development* of attitudes and values, not to encourage the formation of any one particular attitude or value.

Suggested Activities

1. If you have service-learning courses on your campus, provide a list of these courses to your students. Discuss what is involved (e.g., subject, time, credit, location) and possible benefits from matriculating in them. Give an example of how one of these courses may help students explore a particular career area they might be considering.

2. Invite a panel of students from your campus who have been engaged in "experiential learning" activities (both volunteer and service-learning), and ask them to describe their experiences, relay their impressions of the value they received from their involvement, and their recommendations to other students who are considering this option.

Distance Learning
M. Governati, G. Steele, and K. Carey

Distance learning, like service-learning, is very much a part of higher education today. Even many older adult students are not aware of this vehicle for taking courses or obtaining a degree. Younger students need to be aware of this way of learning, if not for the present, at least as a future option. New technologies are continually improving how distance learning is delivered, and innovative curricular designs are improving the experience. The barriers of time and place no longer exist, and a global approach to teaching and learning will lead to many new ways of delivering formal and informal educational practices. This essay describes the current methods by which people can learn through technology. The authors challenge the reader to consider how learning will change in the future because of it.

Discussion Questions

1. What is the difference between synchronous and asynchronous learning?

    Synchronous learning may be viewed as the traditional approach to learning that occurs in the same time and place. Traditional education, for example, is taught in traditional classroom settings. Asynchronous learning, however, can occur anywhere, anytime. The old "correspondence courses" which began at the beginning of the last century, were a form of distance learning taught via the postal service. The Internet, however, has created a whole new context for higher education and many institutions now offer distance learning in some form. Lifetime learning, whether for personal or work-related reasons, will take many new directions as technology makes the acquisition of knowledge available any place, anytime.

2. Should economic considerations be the primary way to evaluate the value of higher education?

    The value of a liberal education has rarely been disputed. In the last century the purpose of a college education was increasingly purported by students (and their parents) to prepare them for an interesting and financially rewarding career. Some futurists think the emphasis of education will shift to the acquisition of knowledge, not only for career purposes, but for a lifetime of learning.

3. Can society afford to let some of its members not participate in distance learning? What would be the costs?

    While there will always be a need and demand for traditional residential colleges where traditional age students will be taught, there will also be a need for more nontraditional modes of teaching and learning. The "digital divide" is considered a serious national issue by some. According to the U.S. Department of

Commerce, 41 percent of all U.S. homes use the Web but only 19 of Black homes and 16 percent of Hispanic homes do. This leaves a large portion of students who will not be prepared for the opportunities that this technology provides. Students who do not have this access must use other resources such as schools and libraries. Society will suffer if the "digital divide" is allowed to continue.

Suggested Activities

1. Take the class to your computer center and have them experience a distance learning course taught on your campus (or demonstrate in the classroom if facilities are available). Discuss their impressions of learning in this way.

2. Invite the distance learning coordinator or a distance learning course instructor on your campus to class to discuss the type of students who sign up for these courses, enrollment procedures, the instructors' expectations, and other pertinent information concerning distance learning.

What Makes a Successful Online Student?
Illinois Online Network

This article briefly summarizes ten unique qualities that a successful online student should possess. It is apparent from this list that some students may not learn best via the virtual classroom. Rating themselves on these ten qualities can help students decide if they are good candidates for and could benefit from distance learning experiences.

Discussion Questions

1. Why is commitment critical to the success of an online student?

    A commitment to learning in this way is essential since students must stay current with the class and complete all the assigned work in the time allotted without the benefit of a classroom structure. Some students with poor study habits may find they are ill suited to this type of learning situation. Students who matriculate in online courses must invest themselves wholeheartedly since failure to commit themselves to the demands of independent learning and closely structured time may work against them.

2. How do you think social interaction might differ in doing a class project from an online course versus a traditional classroom version?

    Good writing skills and interesting ways of communicating their views are especially important if one is "conversing" online. The online student does not see his or her peers, thus biases are not based on physical appearances. Introverts may prefer this type of interaction; individuals who enjoy interacting socially in person, may prefer the traditional classroom method of learning.

Suggested Activity

Give students the Web address of your state's education department and ask them to explore different online courses offered by some of the institutions in your state.

UNIT 5

WHAT ABOUT TECHNOLOGY?

This unit on technology, like Unit 4, was added to this second edition because of the amazing amount of influence technology has had on higher education in the recent past as well as its continuing impact. Although college students have grown up in a computerized world, it is important that they also reflect on its impact on society in general and their own futures in particular. We often take for granted the constant changes in technology, and how they affect our lifestyle and our perceptions of the world around us. The essays in this unit will help to stimulate discussion on how technology not only affects college student life, but its influence on life outside the campus gate.

UNIT 5 READINGS

The Time of Our Lives
Mortimer B. Zuckerman

This reading reviews the many changes that have taken place in society because of technological advances. Zuckerman captures in this essay the essence of change and how this country has developed because of its unique educational system. He describes why the United States is well positioned to deal with the global economy because its past was future-oriented. Zuckerman emphasizes that the American dream of our ancestors still lives as we begin a new century.

Discussion Questions

1. What inventions does Zuckerman say laid the foundation for our modern world? What others, if any, would you add to the list?

    Zuckerman describes the work of the Wright brothers, Edison, Bell, and Marconi as contributing to the foundation of the modern world. Although no one individual is credited with the invention of the computer (the ancient abacus is sometimes referred to as the first computer), it certainly has had a profound impact on our lives. It is difficult to identify all the new technological advances that have resulted just from the invention of a small computer chip.

2. What are the four societies that have emerged in this country? What makes the latest one different from the other three?

    Zuckerman lists the rural agricultural society, the industrial economy, the service economy, and the present information-based economy. Zuckerman describes how the movement to this new economy occurred in phases. The middle class, for example, expanded and the inclusion of past disenfranchised populations became common. Our current economy is a global one. Change has accelerated to a pace unbelievable in past societies.

3. How have "free and universal" educational opportunities affected American progress? How has the role of public education changed over time?

    Zuckerman calls the American educational system unique because high school was not just for the privileged elite but for an increasingly broader segment of the population. He describes the seeds of this movement by giving credit to the turn-of-the-century American philosophers, William James, Lester

Ward, and John Dewey. They espoused education for the masses that eliminated the artificial barriers of wealth and class and led to opportunities for upward mobility. By the end of the century higher education had become the right of every American. He credits the vast network of universities, corporate laboratories, and private and public foundations with integrating new knowledge into practical applications.

4. According to Zuckerman, the United States is uniquely suited to dominate the information age. Why is this so?

    Our democratized capital markets allocate money to the future, not the past, to the new, not the old. Even small businesses can benefit from new technologies. American culture's legacy of individualism, entrepreneurialism, and pragmatism is open to the energy and talent rising from diverse types of individuals. We have the capacity to respond to huge markets, diverse populations, and changing economic conditions. We make decisions based on science and statistics. We have giant systems that help manage technological revolutions, and logistical systems that can handle dynamic, rapidly changing, and complex processes. Zuckerman lists many other reasons why we are so suited to dominate the information age. We are a society that values individualism and the great achievements that have been accomplished because of it.

Suggested Activities

1. Divide the class into small groups. Ask them to project how technology might advance in ten years and how it might affect their lives in the following areas: health, workplace, transportation, education. (Add or substitute your own areas of interest.) Ask each group to share their ideas and discuss how their future lives may change.

2. Ask students to interview persons from the World War II (70-80 years of age), Boomer (35-50 years of age), and X (20-35 years of age) generations to determine how technology has affected their lives, compared to life before. Discuss in class how generational responses from the interviews differed. Ask students how technology affects their lives specifically as students. (If there are representatives in the class from more than one generation, invite them to discuss their impressions.)

An Interview with John Seely Brown
Larry King

John Seely Brown's portrait of the future office he calls a "workscape" offers an interesting picture of how many workers of tomorrow will interact with their physical space. Working takes place over the entire physical space we traverse in a single day. This workscape's requirements have many implications for the type of skills students will need to develop, especially in the areas of communications and interpersonal relationships. Brown's description of a "totally integrated communication appliance" suggests how dramatically technology will change time and space. He also discusses other issues that will affect the future "workscape" such as the need to understand multiculturalism, security, the need for a new type of organizational architect, and new kinds of "bosses," to mention a few that students might find useful to discuss.

Discussion Questions

1. Why does John Seely Brown use the term "workscape" instead of "office" for describing the 21st century workplace? What does he mean by "meeting capture tools"?

   We will no longer be confined to one location in the future workplace. The term "workscape" describes the entire physical space through which we travel during our workday, including highways, airports, conference rooms, and home. "Meeting capture tools" include many innovative ways of recording and later using what is said in a meeting. These tools will integrate discussions and decision making automatically; they can be used during the meeting or for recording purposes later.

2. What is "IP addressable," and how will it be different from what we now use?

   All electronic devices that are used by a worker will be integrated through a connection to the Internet and many functions will be carried on at the same time. Brown describes a wireless device that integrates all functions with high-resolution displays, and possibly a virtual keyboard.

3. How will the global economy affect the type of staff needed in the new workscape?

   Brown describes a staff member who understands multiculturalism, be it bilingual or bicultural. Not only will they be language translators, but also they will be "meaning" translators so every point of view is understood as intended.

4. How might the new workscape affect the family?

   The new workscape will be more family-friendly. Since the boundaries between living, working, and learning will not be so rigid, the presence of family members will not be unusual. The physical dangers of the workplace will not exist in knowledge-work, so that barrier will not bar family members from the workscape.

5. How does the author describe a "learning culture," and why is it so important? What is a "knowledge artist," and how could you become one?

   One's ability to learn will be key in the competitive world of the 21st century. Willingness to learn and interest in learning (e.g., learning new skills every three to five years) will be imperative. According to Brown, learning is a social activity. Physical spaces, social spaces, and informational spaces will need to be reformed in a way that enhances learning. Knowledge artists will be involved in creative activities that form content in many contexts, including media. They will bring their artistic sensitivities to areas where complex knowledge needs to be understood, such as Web sites. They will be able to make a complex idea beautifully simple through their artistic skills that creatively present content.

Suggested Activities

1. Ask students to discuss their ideal work environment. What type of workscape would they prefer not to work in?

2. Invite a retailer to class to demonstrate the very latest technological gadgets (e.g., palm pilots, phones, Internet connections) that are on the market. Ask them to project the type of products that will be available in the near future.

Virtual Legality: An Overview of
Your Rights and Responsibilities in Cyberspace
Steven J. McDonald

Although today's college students are very familiar with the Internet and its varied applications, many are unfamiliar with the legal issues surrounding its use. This essay describes many areas of use or misuse on college campuses. The legal issues that college students may encounter in using the Internet are outlined and suggestions for avoiding common legal problems are presented in a clear and concise manner.

Discussion Questions

1. Why, according to the author, does the Internet have such potential for misuse?

    Many Internet users are unaware of the unlimited audience who has access to their postings. Free speech is often mistakenly thought to include whatever is technically possible. It is the computer user's responsibility to know and comply with the restrictions placed by your institution's computer systems and networks.

2. How does the author suggest you can judge what is legal or illegal in cyberspace?

    Since the same laws and policies apply to cyberspace that they do in the "offline" world, they are not exempt from the normal requirements of legal and ethical behavior. Computer users who engage in electronic communications with persons in other states or countries are subject to the laws governing those systems and networks as well.

3. How do copyright laws affect the Internet?

    Placing a work on the Internet does not mean it is automatically in the public domain. As soon as an e-mail message, Usenet posting, web page, or other work is seen, it is copyrighted. As with any copyrighted work, it may not be used unless the owner has given permission, it is in the public domain, "fair use" is constituted, or an "implied license" is given. The application of copyright laws to the Internet, however, is still not completely clear, but using some common sense guidelines outlined by the author will help students avoid possible problems.

4. Why is your online "right to privacy" so important?

    No one has the right to invade your privacy without your authorization. Invasion of privacy is considered a "tort" which means you can be sued for monetary damages. It is illegal for personal information to be given about an individual if there is no legitimate need or reason to know.

5. Why are "hacking," or "cracking," and similar activities illegal?

    Accessing, using, or altering data on a computer without proper authorization, transmitting computer viruses over networks, conducting "e-mail bombing," or similar activities are illegal. Engaging in these activities may harm people and makes you liable for monetary damages.

Suggested Activities

1. Invite someone from your computer center to class to discuss the legal implications outlined in this essay as they pertain to your campus and its computer operations.

2. Ask an expert in "privacy" laws to discuss with the class how to avoid becoming a "victim" of Internet fraud.

The Connected Library
Clifford Stoll

Although written in a somewhat humorous style, in this essay Stoll presents his serious views on what is happening in the library he frequents as well as libraries in general. He complains about "appearance over function." He bemoans the disappearance of bookshelves full of books that have been shipped for storage to a warehouse miles away. He accuses technologists (who have often replaced librarians) of changing libraries into "sterile information warehouses." Discussing the changes students have seen in your campus library may support Stoll's frustration, or laud the use of technology to bring libraries into the 21st century.

Discussion Questions

1. What do you think of the writing style the author uses to share his view of the current direction of libraries?

    The cynicism that Stoll uses to make his point about the changing library may strengthen his argument in some people's minds. His opinions, while couched in humor, are presented in a way that forcibly makes his point.

2. What does the author claim is happening to our library systems in general?

    They are "riding the information age bandwagon." Books are being replaced with computers and other technological "gizmos" that will become obsolete within a short period of time. Librarians have become information specialists rather than stewards of books; from stewards of our cultural endowment to professional information handlers. The number of books being purchased has decreased since more of the budget is being spent on technology.

3. The author is assessing his library system based on his need for research functions. Are there other functions for which the automated library might be more useful and effective?

    While one of the functions of a campus library is to supply the resources for researching information about any subject, a well-equipped library with state-of-the-art technology offers a different type of resource to which some students do not have access. In this technological age, computerized searches provide the most immediate and current access to information that would not appear in printed form for many months or even years. Libraries provide access to the Internet that would not be available to some students and other library patrons. A library also provides an environment that is conducive to study for some students who seek a quiet haven.

4. Upon what does the author base his opinion about the obsolescence of tomorrow's libraries?

    He is basing his opinions on his observations of what is happening in his campus library (i.e., empty carrels, broken and unused ethernet ports). He also conducted an unsystematic survey of pedestrians on a street who supported his contention that there should be books in a library.

Suggested Activities

1. Ask a group of students to conduct a survey of your campus library. What percentage of students are using some type of technology and what percentage is using books and other printed material in the library?

2. Invite your campus librarian into class to discuss the role he or she plays as a librarian. What technological resources does your library offer students? Give your librarian a copy of the reading by O'Hanlon in Unit 3 before the class meets. Ask him or her to relate the research suggestions in that reading to your campus library system.

Technology Eliminating Conversation
Ellen Goodman

Ellen Goodman describes how new telephone technology has changed her life in ways she never dreamed possible. Like many, she is still surprised at how well she has adapted to this new way of communicating, even though she is not sure she likes it.

Discussion Questions

1. How does Ellen Goodman compare her current involvement with technology with her past experiences?

    Goodman remembers when a telephone was a "beloved instrument of conversation" and courtesy was a virtue. Now Goodman says she feels like a "target of snipers" since so many machines are pointed at her.

2. What is the "new etiquette" associated with increased telephone technology, according to the author?

    The new etiquette, according to Goodman, is to dodge phone calls. To be out of touch directly is the current mode of communicating. Talking to people directly has been replaced with leaving a message so one-to-one conversations can be eliminated.

3. What does the author mean by "efficiency trumps courtesy"?

    She says we now use the phone as a "drop-off center." The old fashion courtesy of answering the phone when it rings has been replaced with impersonal, avoidance tactics for which we actually pay on our phone bill.

Suggested Activity

Discuss with students how phone etiquette has changed with the advent of the mobile phone and other phone related technological inventions. Should a new approach to telephone etiquette be established for today's telephone users?

UNIT 6

WHAT SHOULD I KNOW ABOUT CAREERS?

Since one of the main reasons students give for wanting a college degree is to enhance their chances for "finding a job" that is going to challenge them and help them be "better off financially," the readings in this Unit should be of great interest to them. Discussion can include how they can prepare practically for the workplace. It is equally important for them to clarify their personal work values and define the meaning of "career" in all aspects of their lives. Since many students narrowly equate their choice of major with the career opportunities to which it can lead, thinking about "career" in broader terms can perhaps alleviate some of the pressures that first year students, in particular, feel about making the right initial educational and vocational choices.

UNIT 6 READINGS

Getting a Living
Henry David Thoreau

This essay offers a glimpse of Thoreau's work values for the time and day he lived. Students can discuss how these values are the same or different today considering the complexity of our society as compared to America in the 1860's. How have the basic tasks of farm workers or other laborers changed from Thoreau's time to our own? Are the students' work values similar or different?

Discussion Questions

1. How does Thoreau define "meaningless labor"?

    He defines it as labor that he perceives as "make-up" work with no purpose except to satisfy one's desire for money (or to move a heavy stone for esthetic purposes). What do students think of as "meaningless work"?

2. How is his perception of work different from the others in his town?

    Thoreau considered thinking and writing as "work" but he doubts whether others in his town would consider it so since there was no bustle of activity or no tangible product produced or sold. Can a writer fool people as easily as those engaged in commerce or other professions?

3. What is Thoreau's opinion of money?

    He claims that the jobs that pay money are "disagreeable to render." Whenever he has offered his services for money, such as surveying or inventing a rule for measuring cord-wood, employers are not interested in the correct way but how it will best benefit them. To be a successful writer or lecturer in his day, one must be popular, which led to taking money for saying what people wanted to hear, not necessarily what Thoreau wanted to say. Has anything changed in this regard since Thoreau's time?

4. What does Thoreau say about work that is performed well versus work that provides a living?

    Thoreau thinks that when people work they should concentrate on working well, rather than thinking about the money they are making. In the end, if workers did not have to think about money, perhaps they would be more inclined to work "for the love of it." Do students think this philosophy would work today? Do they think it worked in Thoreau's time? What would be their attitude working in a job they didn't like? In one they did?

5. If Thoreau were to give a lecture on your college campus, would the students attend? What questions would they like to ask him?

Thoreau was writing in a context, but that context has greatly changed. Encourage students to discuss the ways in which they think social and commercial practices have changed since Thoreau's day.

Suggested Activities

1. Ask students to form two groups based on their agreement or disagreement with Thoreau's statement that "the way by which you may get money can only lead downward." After they have discussed their point of view, ask the two sides to state their position and then debate which side has made a more substantial case.

2. Suggest to students that they read the entire essay, *"Life Without Principle,"* the speech from which the above reading was extracted, or *Walden* in which Thoreau writes more about his philosophy of work..

Job Search: Chance or Plan?
Mark R. Ballard

This essay contains many practical tips for preparing for the job search during the college years. Many students make the mistake that "Terry" made and think that finding a job is something that you begin your senior year or after graduation. This approach can be disastrous in today's job market. Knowing how to approach the job-search process in a timely and orderly way can help students feel confident of their ability to find a position that fulfills their interests and potential.

Discussion Questions

1. What is the first important step in the job search process, according to Ballard?

   The first step, which begins during the freshman year, is to assess your interests, abilities, values, and other personal characteristics. Only when you begin to explore those qualities that make you a unique individual can you begin to examine academic and occupational possibilities that would suit you. Ask students if they know where on your campus they can get help with this selfexploration.

2. What would you tell an employer about yourself in thirty minutes during a job interview?

   Ask students to make a list of personal information that they might tell an employer. How difficult is this task? Where are there weak spots in this information (e.g., few work experiences, lack of communication skills, lack of references)? Can they make a "dream" list of how they would like it to look like their senior year? What can they do to start accomplishing this?

3. What are the six steps that Ballard outlines to systematically begin the career planning process?

   Go over each of the six steps that are listed in the reading. Ask students where on campus they can receive help with each of these steps. Who outside of campus can help them with these tasks? Why are these steps so important and why should students follow them in the order given?

4. What type of work experiences can students engage in prior to graduation?

   Work experience can be obtained through part-time jobs, volunteer work, and student activities. Cooperative education and internships, however, are more beneficial since employers will see they have been involved in real work settings with supervision. They will also have been formally evaluated by their employers.

5. What are some strategies students can use during their freshman year to enhance the career planning process? As sophomores? Juniors? Seniors?

   Ballard's list of tasks geared specifically to each year can provide an outline from which students can plan. Ask students if they have completed the tasks associated with their particular year in school. How can freshmen, in particular, use Ballard's list to insure they will be prepared to enter the job market at the time they graduate?

Suggested Activities

1. Ask students to pay a visit to the Career Services Office on your campus and write a brief report on resources they found there to help them with career decision making and job search activities. OR Invite a professional from the Career Services Office on your campus to speak to the class about the services they provide. Be sure to give your speaker a copy of the Ballard essay prior to class so he or she can strengthen or add to some of the points made.

2. Ask students to put together two resumes: One that reflects the type of work experiences they have had up to now, and one that describes what they would like to accomplish by the time they graduate. Ask students to compare the two and list some actions that they can take while they are in college to develop the one that they want as seniors.

Postgraduate Paralysis
Mary Sherry

This essay describes the dilemma of many college graduates who do not follow the advice given in the previous reading by Ballard. It also offers a picture of parents' frustration when they watch their son or daughter struggle to find a job after college. Students can share the experiences of siblings or other students who have graduated without a position and those who do. What has been the difference in the job search activities between those who have a job and those who don't? How do students feel about being "underemployed" after graduation?

Discussion Questions

1.   Why do some students feel like failures if they do not have a job at graduation, according to Sherry?

They feel they have "done all the right things," but they are not able to begin a "career." They were not offered fat salaries and generous benefits. They were not offered the "perfect job." Students might want to discuss what their expectations are for a job after graduation. How will they feel if they do all the right things and then can't find their dream job? Are they willing to take an entry-level job that may not be what they had hoped for but one that will provide valuable experience?

2.   How did Sherry's daughter approach the job-search process?

She was looking for a career, not a job. She was looking for a position that would meet her expectations of a job that in reality only comes after considerable time and experience. What kinds of "entry-level jobs" can students identify?

3.   What is the difference between a job and a career?

A career is an "evolutionary process" that takes many years and includes all aspects of life, including work as a volunteer and other related experiences. A series of jobs can in time build to a career in a specific field. Since most people will change jobs six to eight times and careers several times during their lives (according to the Department of Labor), students need to learn that their career is a life-long journey.

4.   What advice does Sherry give for finding entry-level jobs?

Graduates need to "pound the pavement." Do students think this is good advice? How often do graduates without a job "give up" and apply for graduate or professional school because they do not find the kind of position that is up to their expectations?

5.   How did Sherry's daughter finally find her first job? Subsequent jobs?

She used a head-hunter who helped her assess her skills and prepare for interviews. She answered different types of ads. For subsequent jobs she used head-hunters, want ads, friends, and business contacts that she had made from her previous jobs. How does this advice differ from or complement Ballard's suggestions?

Suggested Activities

1. Suggest to students that they talk with at least two recent college graduates who are currently employed. How did they prepare themselves for the job market? What did these graduates wish they had done while in college to enhance their chances of finding a satisfying position after graduation? What advice do they have for the students in selecting a major and preparing for the job market?

2. Ask students to write a brief essay on the differences between a job and a career and discuss why it is important to make this distinction during college and when they graduate.

Virtual Organization
Samuel E. Bleecker

Since many students, even non-business majors, will work for corporations, this reading will help them understand how businesses are changing. In this essay, Bleecker describes a virtual organization, or a business that will be defined by collaborative networks that will include thousands of workers who are bound by a common purpose. These "operations without walls" are possible because of increasingly sophisticated technologies that are able to collapse time and space. The reshaped corporation of the future, according to Bleecker, will depend on communication rather than location.

Discussion Questions

1. According to Bleecker, how are corporations changing into "virtual organizations"?

   Corporations are evolving and will continue to evolve in decades to come. Rather than being defined by concrete walls and physical space, they are formed from combinations of computer and communication networks that allow them to link thousands of workers who can be working from any geographical location.

2. What does Bleecker mean by operating "without walls"?

   The collaborative networks that make up the virtual organization operate from any location, dispensing with the need for workers to be located in one office or building.

3. What are the four virtual trends in the marketplace that Bleecker describes, and how do they encourage "virtual enterprising"?

   The four trends include pace, cost, personalization, and globalization. The pace of business is escalating and competition is often based on how fast a business can respond to the market. The startup costs of businesses are lower because of these technological advances. Customer demands are easier to respond to due to computerized manufacturing. Businesses now compete internationally rather than locally as before.

4. How does the author describe "mobile knowledge worker"?

   The author points out that today the "office is where the worker is," which is different from the past. Mobile knowledge workers spend more time on the road than at their desks because they can stay in touch by phone, computer, fax, pager, or videoconference. As this continues it will require the development of increasingly sophisticated wireless tools and virtual networks. The "road warrior" will have a universal mailbox.

5. What is "warware," and what is its function?

   "Warware" is strategic simulation software that will allow managers to artificially imitate business scenarios free of risk. They will be able to simulate projects to predict results based on the testing of different solutions.

6. Who is Alvin Toffler, and why is he mentioned in this essay?

Alvin Toffler is a futurist who has written many books predicting events that will take place in every aspect of society and how our lives might be affected by these future events. Toffler is quoted in this reading because many of the predictions he has made about business and other parts of society have come true.

Suggested Activities

1. Review the reading in Unit 5 by Larry King in which he interviews John Seely Brown about the office of the future. Ask students to discuss the ideas generated by the two readings and how they feel about working in the types of work environments that these two writers describe.

2. Ask students to write a brief review of a book, magazine article, or Internet site that is futuristic in nature. (For example, the *Futurist* magazine or www.wfs.com.)

Career Patterns for the 21st Century
Peggy Simonsen

We have seen many different types of career paths emerge in the past decade because of the changes in how the workplace functions. Simonsen describes how workers are beginning to control their own career paths, rather than under the control of an employer. The traditional linear, upward career path will no longer be the norm. There will be greater flexibility in the future for the way individuals control how and where they work.

Discussion Questions

1. In what ways do these new career patterns differ from the old, more traditional ones?

   The traditional career path of the past rewarded workers by "moving them up" in the organization and rewarding them with automatic raises and other perks such as their own parking space. There are many new career patterns that have different expectations and rewards. Individuals will make career choices based on what is best for them rather than relying on an employer to move them "up the ladder."

2. What, according to Simonsen, are the characteristics of the "life-style" career pattern?

   Excessive work demands often take time from family and other interests that are a priority for some workers. Individuals who prefer the "life-style" pattern admit career is important, but prefer a balanced life based on their total life needs. Two-career households have often deprived couples of time together, so this pattern is increasing as priorities are weighed in favor of family responsibilities.

3. How do modern linear careers differ from those in the past?

   Rather than spending one's whole working life in one organization, modern linear careers see workers changing jobs when they reach a plateau or growth slows. Employers will no longer be able to take a worker's commitment to a job for granted. People who build linear careers today will take a broader organizational perspective rather than a personally driven perspective, according to Simonsen. Promotions will be based on ability to lead. People attracted to linear careers are motivated by achievement, power, ambition, and define success in their own way.

4. Why might an "expert career pattern" be difficult to maintain in work that changes rapidly?

   The rapid changes in the workplace will require "experts" to continuously develop their expertise. Maintaining a level of expertise that needs to change as the demand for certain competencies change is not simple. For example, organizational priorities might change in response to market demands, so the expert's particular expertise might not be applicable or needed in this new milieu.

5. Why are younger people purposely building sequential careers, according to Simonsen?

   A sequential career means workers are free to make choices in the type of work they wish to do at different points in their lives. Some people prefer a variety of work experiences and if a job is boring or no longer challenging, they feel free to move to another job to pursue another area of interest. They like change, challenges, and variety. The thought of the traditional linear career is not appealing to them.

Suggested Activities

1. Invite a panel of workers who represent several of the career patterns that Simonsen describes and ask them to share their experiences with the students.

2. Give the students a list of work values (if you do not have one, ask your counseling or career center for one) and ask students to select the values that are most likely held by workers in the patterns that Simonsen describes. Discuss how their own work values might lead them to a certain career pattern.

UNIT 7

WHAT ARE MY RIGHTS AND RESPONSIBILITIES AS A STUDENT?

For most people, the four or five years after high school graduation are a time for defining and strengthening personal values. Institutions of higher education provide a special environment for this process of definition, for they, as part of their essential nature, are defined by values inherent in freedom of inquiry, ideas, and the search for truth.

UNIT 7 READINGS

On Academic Freedom
William H. Halverson and James R. Carter

In one of the most traditionally philosophical essays in this collection, Halverson and Carter argue that humans create institutions to serve specific functions, and that the reason for which universities were created is the search for and discovery of truth. This search can be successful only in an environment that defends the freedom to voice and to evaluate critically every point of view. Such an environment is said to enjoy "academic freedom." The authors also identify common barriers to academic freedom to which individuals need to be alert, in order to protect this essential characteristic of higher education.

Discussion Questions

1. Identify and explain the paradox in the statement, "the surest way to establish the truth of an assertion is to try to disprove it."

    The paradox is that the harder we unsuccessfully labor to disprove an assertion, the stronger a true assertion will show itself to be. This paradox is true because false assertions can be shown to be false only when they are exposed to public view and criticism. The longer an assertion can hold up against the onslaught of critical attack, the likelier it is to be a true assertion.

2. What, according to Halverson and Carter, are the two necessary conditions without which academic freedom cannot exist?

    First, academic freedom can exist "only in a community of open and intelligent individuals who recognize that in principle every legitimate question deserves an answer, and that the legitimacy of question and answer cannot be assumed but must be shown capable of withstanding criticism." Second, "academic freedom requires that this community make truth its common purpose, and free and open discussion the means to it."

3. Halverson and Carter argue that "one who desires to know the truth concerning any matter must be persuaded by the evidence, and by the evidence alone." What else are people persuaded by?

    An old adage says that "might makes right" and many people believe versions of this saying when, for example, they respect the ideas of rich people more than the ideas of poor people, in spite of the fact that the value of an idea has nothing to do with the value of its source. Similarly, people sometimes respect older or traditional ideas because of their age, not for their intrinsic truth.

People are often misled when they believe what they would like to be true rather than what they can prove to be true. Such errors are often related to culture and family: when we find that others hold beliefs that are different from ours, we tend to explain the difference and justify our beliefs because they are shared by our family or in our culture and not shared by others.

4. What, according to Halverson and Carter, are the enemies of academic freedom?

    Halverson and Carter identify internal and external enemies of academic freedom. Internal enemies include our fear of new ideas because of the comfort we have in staying with our old ideas; sheer laziness, because it is easier to accept a received view than puzzle one out for ourselves; and undue respect for tradition, when evidence should outweigh tradition. External enemies of academic freedom include any kind of force used to compel agreement and discourage free inquiry.

5. How, according to Halverson and Carter, should we regard the opinions we have received from people we respect?

    They say, "the opinions of one's forebears deserve considerable respect for they represent the acquired wisdom of many generations. Still we must not be bound by them, and we must be willing to abandon them if the weight of available evidence suggests that they are mistaken." For example, nineteenth century Americans mistrusted the new automobile, because they believed that to travel faster than 15 miles per hour would cause fatal nosebleeds and brain hemorrhages. This belief died only when evidence could be brought to bear to show that it was false.

Suggested Activities

1. Invite students to identify a small number of important issues (abortion, legalizing drug use, gays in the military, higher education as an end in itself or as a mean to an end) and then to select one issue from their list for a class debate. On their chosen issue, formulate a specific topic: e.g., "Abortion should not permitted except in the case of demonstrable threat to the life of the mother" or "Abortion is a personal matter, since every woman has the right to control over her own body."

    Once you have identified such a topic statement, ask students to divide between those who are generally (or loosely) in favor and those who are against. Then gently control a discussion (one speaker for, one against) until you have some evidence in hand. Are students swayed only by the evidence, or are there enemies to academic freedom at work in their points of view?

2. Assign students to write a brief essay about an issue on which they have recently changed their minds, and why; or on a belief they hold strongly and what would be required as evidence for them to question or change their belief.

The New Immorality
Joseph Wood Krutch

Krutch asks whether it is true, as it sometimes seems to him, that public morality is rising while private morality is on the decline. Since he cannot measure public and private morality precisely, he cites examples that seem persuasive to him and avoids any absolute conclusion except the assertion that if only one individual believes in personal honor and acts on that belief while all others seem to have abandoned it, then "at least he will still retain what is perhaps the most important part of humanity."

Discussion Questions

1. Define "honor" as you think Krutch means it.

    For Krutch, "honor" seems to mean a personal, interior sense of what is right and wrong, and the determination to follow that personal sense.

2. What does Krutch mean by the sentence, "I hold that it is indeed inevitable that the so-called social conscience unsupported by the concept of personal honor will create a corrupt society"?

    Krutch is concerned with the beliefs and actions of society, but he argues that the individuals in any society are ultimately the source of ethical or moral action, and that unless the society is composed of good persons--that is, persons of honor, then that society as an aggregate cannot be a good society. The individual's personal sense of honor is at the core of social good.

3. How might you attempt to answer the question: "Is there really any evidence that personal dishonesty is more prevalent than it always was?" How does Krutch attempt to answer it?

    Social scientists who study student behavior might try to answer this question by administering the same survey to many succeeding generations of college students and comparing the results of those surveys. Such surveys are generally limited to self-reported information and are based on perceptions rather than actions.

    Another measure would be to contact the "Honor" offices of many colleges and ask how many cases of suspected misconduct have been sent forward to them by members of their faculty, year by year.

    Krutch recognizes that he lacks genuinely objective measures that would prove or disprove this statement. He writes: "I have no way of making a historical measurement. Perhaps these things are not actually more prevalent. What I do know" [here, Krutch relies on his own experience. and reading] "is that there is an increasing tendency to accept and take for granted such personal dishonesty."

4. Underlying Krutch's beliefs as expressed in this essay is the insistence that "for the individual himself nothing is more important than this personal, interior sense of right and wrong." Others might respond that such an interior sense is learned from those around us and therefore that different cultures are likely to result in different "personal, interior" senses of right and wrong. Which of these positions do you agree with? Why?

    In answering this question, students should be encouraged to take a stand on one side or the other and hold a civilized debate. It can be especially interesting to have older, "nontraditional" students participate in such a discussion, since they are likelier to have come into contact with persons who differ from themselves in ethics and experience.

5. What does Krutch mean by the assertion that "Only he who possesses himself and is content with himself is actually secure"?

Krutch raises the issue of security in order to identify the sources of true security within ourselves. Do we depend on material riches? We can lose them swiftly. Do we depend on how others regard us for our own sense of value? Others can die or depart from us, or they can be wrong in the way they perceive and judge us.

Each of us has for certain only himself or herself to depend upon, since the only person sure to be with you from birth to death is you yourself. "Know thyself," the persistent motto of Renaissance thought, underlies Krutch's assertion, since before we can be content with ourselves, each of us needs to know who he or she is. Once we know ourselves, we have to be willing to act on our own sense of moral judgment rather than merely to follow the crowd. Knowing yourself and acting upon what you know of yourself is, for Krutch, the foundation of security.

Suggested Activities

1. Invite students to identify actions which they took against the advice of their friends or members of their family. Did those actions have an ethical component? If so, of what kind? (For example, did they result in benefit or harm to others?) Were their actions motivated by a personal sense of honor or by some other factor?

2. Among college students of almost every generation, a significant cause of unethical behavior is the abuse of alcohol. Assign students to write a theme (1) defining the "abuse" of alcohol and (2) identifying a plan to discourage such abuse on your campus.

Ideas as Property
Thomas L. Minnick

We generally understand physical things that we own to be our property and recognize their theft as a crime against us. Minnick argues that our ideas are equally to be considered as property and the theft of them to be regarded as serious, especially in a college or university setting. Since the search for true ideas is part of the mission of higher education, protecting those ideas from theft is essential work in every college and university. An institution shows its dedication to valuing ideas by establishing and disseminating rules and safeguards for the protection of ideas as property. The conventional usage of footnotes and bibliography help to conserve an author's ownership of an idea, and so does an institution's seriousness in dealing with instances of academic theft.

Discussion Questions

1.   What is the historical basis for "ownership of property"?

        One of our oldest root ideas is the notion of property owned by individuals or a group (such as a tribe or clan). This idea underlies our system of money and barter: why trade cash or goods and services for something unless it belongs to someone else? It also underlies our idea of theft, since no one can steal from you unless you own something, and they can steal only the thing you own.

2. How does the author define "ideas as property"? How do ideas and material property differ?

        Ideas are like material property in many ways. For example, some ideas generate cash and are therefore the source of material property: the people who invented Teflon or Xerox or Post-it notes should all be wealthy, if they were wise enough to retain their property interest in their own ideas. Any single item of material property can be owned only by one entity (whether a person, like Henry Ford, or a group of people, like all Ford Company stockholders). But any idea can be simultaneously possessed by everyone who understands it. Giving away material property means you don't have it any more. But you can share an idea with the world, and then everyone will have that idea.

3.   Why is the concept of ideas a property so important in a university setting?

        Ideas are the lifeblood of a university or college. Students are graded on the quality of their ideas, and staff and faculty members are rewarded for good ideas and (sometimes) punished for bad ones. The quality of a college or university, more than any other single man-made institution, depends on the quality of the ideas which comprise it. So protecting those ideas matters more in an educational setting than almost anywhere else.

4. What steps can be taken by a university to insure ideas as property are protected, according to the author?

        Minnick says that a school can protect ideas from thieves in three ways. The first step is to make clear to everyone that "ideas are a kind of property, and that the protection of those ideas really does matter to the well-being" of the institution. A second step is to teach students at all levels the conventions for acknowledging when they adopt or develop the ideas of someone else. The third is to deal seriously with instances of the theft of ideas . . . ."

5.   What can happen to a student who is found to have cheated or plagiarized?

Ask students if they know the penalties (sometimes called "sanctions") at your institution for getting caught cheating from the work of another student. These are likely to range from lighter to more severe penalties. For example, at the authors' home institution, a letter of admonition or a course grade of "Failed" will be imposed for a first offence or for a first-year student, while suspension or dismissal almost always follow a second verdict of Guilty. Then ask students if they believe that there might be internal consequences to acts of cheating or plagiarism.

Suggested Activities

1. Ask students to name a variety of acts of academic misconduct--such as cheating on a major examination by using crib notes, cheating on that same examination by looking at a neighbor's answers and paraphrasing them, copying someone's history assignment, and the like. Then ask them to name some offenses against material property--such as stealing someone's history textbook and selling it back to the bookstore, or stealing a car. Then invite the class to rank these offenses from "most serious" to "least serious." As each ranking is proposed, require students to defend or contradict it.

2.Invite three or four students each to select one of the common conventions for citing prior publications (Turabian, MLA Style, Chicago Style, APA Style, etc.) and present the essentials of their chosen pattern to the class.

Please Stop This Talk About Values
George F. Will

George Will identifies talk about "values" as a relatively recent phenomenon, and he says that the popularity of talk about values has to do with its non-judgmental character. We all have values: even Hitler and Stalin had values. They valued themselves and their power. But Will wants us to return to old-fashioned talk about virtues. Punctuality, honor, acts of charity to the poor—these are virtuous. Not everyone has virtues, or at least not the same virtues, and some virtues are more important than others. Let's get back to talking about, and aiming to develop, virtues, Will asserts.

Discussion Questions

1. What is the fundamental difference that Will draws between values and virtues? What are his best examples of this difference, in your view? Can you suggest other examples?

    Values are choices, Will says, and anyone can make choices, but virtues are the result of habits, "difficult to develop and therefore not equally accessible to all." Values are whatever you like, whatever "strikes your fancy." Virtues represent excellence—in politics, in poetry, "in science and in faith." The distinction is between doing what you like and doing what you should.

2. Why does Will refer to Lafayette and Washington in his brief essay?

    Will refers to Lafayette first because he is giving a speech at Lafayette College. This reference leads him to others about the Founding Fathers of the United States. He identifies the start of talk about values as 1983, in a speech by British Prime Minister Margaret Thatcher. (It is an irony surely not lost on Will, a conservative political analyst, that values-talk started with a conservative.) And he wants discourse to return to a time before 1983 when virtues were held up as goals in education.

3. Did Hitler have "values," as Will claims. If so, what might they have been?

    One characteristic of Hitler that is frequently mentioned is that he loved his dogs. It is reasonable to say he valued them, and that he valued his notion of the German ideal. He also valued loyalty in his generals. But he also valued a world free of Jews, Roman Catholics, and homosexuals, and he used his power to rid the world of those that he did not value.

Suggested Activities

1. Ask students to give some examples of excellence: excellence in sports, in music, in entertainment (movies, plays), in volunteer service—or any other human activity. (it can be interesting to encourage students to disagree with each on whether a given example is truly "excellent.") Do these examples of excellence have anything in

common? Then ask them to identify the shared causes of that excellence. Are the results "virtues" or is something more needed to earn that name?

2. Is it possible to talk about both values <u>and</u> virtues? Ask students to identify both what they value and the virtues that they may be striving to develop. Are they related?

UNIT 8

WHAT IS DIVERSITY AND WHY IS IT IMPORTANT TO ME?

Sometimes the meaning of a word that is used frequently can become fuzzy or be lost altogether. The word "diversity" is in danger of just such a loss of meaning, since it has become both a political rallying cry and a target. Some faculty members have recently worked to broaden the traditional college curriculum to include courses in the history and content of many diverse contemporary cultures (such as Asian cultures, Hispanic cultures, women's culture, African-American culture and the like). Their efforts, sometimes taken to extremes, have raised criticisms of enforced "political correctness." To such charges, these reformers point out that students will soon need to deal increasingly with many cultures.

Indeed, American students seem truly to live in a transitional period. They live after a time of relative stability, shared values and fixed alliances. They can expect a future in which there is likely to be no majority culture, in which political power will be shared by many more than two "super power" nations, and in which many social units may emerge to replace traditional families and communities. How do colleges and individual students cope in this emerging world? To paraphrase a sentence from the introduction to Unit 8: without abandoning the rich history of Western thought, we value diversity and believe that the free expression of diverse points of view, and positive interactions among diverse cultures, will be essential to the well being of us all in the 21st century. The readings in this unit are meant to lay a foundation for the appreciation of differences among us-- intellectually, culturally, and in many other ways

UNIT 8 READINGS

Fitting In
Betty LaSere Erickson and Diane Weltner Strommer

New first-year students enter higher education with their own priorities, which can and often do differ from those of their parents, teachers, and counselors. Whatever groups students may identify themselves to be part of, one of the highest of their priorities is finding a place to "fit in." Their goal is to feel themselves to be an accepted part of a community that they belong to; and for many students, achieving this goal quickly will lead to academic success and a higher probability of remaining in college through the completion of their program.

Fitting in presents special challenges to students who, as Erickson and Strommer state, "do not match the campus norm." This is true in part because while students in the "campus norm" groups are adjusting to each other, those in groups outside the norm are adjusting to their cohort as well as to the campus majority culture. Populations outside the norm are likely to include disabled students, minority students, international students, gay students, and older nontraditional students. Each of these populations has its own concerns and needs its own sense of accommodation.

Almost all new first-year students need to feel that they can fit in academically. One recent study by P. T. Terenzini and T. M. Wright found that "academic integration" (the feeling of "fitting in" in the academic classroom) had both direct and indirect effects on freshman year reports of personal growth. Indeed, this study suggests that "finding a niche academically, fitting into and succeeding in classes, may have more influence on personal growth . . . than does fitting in socially."

Discussion Questions

1. Adapting to a new environment can mean learning to "fit in" to many new situations. Identify some of these situations that are common to most freshmen.

   No generalization will apply equally to all new first-year students. However, many freshmen will find that they need to make a conscious adjustment to experiences such as living in a residence hall; planning their own time schedule when much of their time is not structured in the way it was likely to be in high school; or planning time to meet the new demands of being in college if the student is older, already has commitments to a job and family, and is squeezing academic work into an already tight schedule; taking responsibility for their own diet; making medical appointments when needed and handling other duties that others used to handle for them; setting priorities that will get the work done; and so on.

   In addition, following the clue provided by Terenzini and Wright, instructors may want to probe for details about what is required as freshmen attempt to adjust academically. How <u>does</u> college mathematics compare with their previous training in math? Ditto for English composition, chemistry, history, and the other courses many first-year students may be taking in common.

2. Many people regard a new environment as unsettling, but a better way may be to think of each new environment as a new opportunity. How can these different points of view affect students' behavior as they attempt to "fit in"?

   The important point about this question is just raising it, since redefining a "problem" as a "challenge" or an "opportunity" may be enough to help students to view it differently and positively. Fitting in can be easier for everyone if attempted in a positive frame of mind. One experienced long-time teacher at Ohio State recently said on a video for new students: "I have found over the years that my most successful students are also likely to be the ones with the most positive outlook."

3. According to Erickson and Strommer, what special problems do minority freshmen face when they attempt to fit in at college?

   Erickson and Strommer point out that minority students are likely to have to adjust to living in two worlds between which there is substantial disparity. Financially disadvantaged students may have come from a high school in which all students had about the same amount of family resources to depend on, but in college a student who rides the bus may be in class next to someone whose parents provided a BMW. This disparity can increase the minority student's sense of isolation. Minority students, especially those in a predominantly white institution, may also have fewer models of success to identify with and fewer natural mentors to turn to, fewer previous on-campus experiences, and fewer peers to join.

4. In general, what is the role of faculty members' in helping students to fit in? Does this have specific implications for minority students?

   In the classroom, say Erickson and Strommer, faculty members create the climate. Overt instances of faculty prejudice will be immediately seen as permission for discriminatory actions and beliefs by students. Some faculty actions take a more subtle form than overt discrimination. For example, faculty members need to be careful to call on minority students as frequently as they call on majority students (however "majority" and "minority" may be defined by the campus context). And the rules that faculty members set sometimes need to take special circumstances into account.

5. Why do Erickson and Strommer consider the results of the study by Terenzini and Wright to be "somewhat surprising"?

    The study by Terenzini and Wright argues that a student's adjustment to the academic demands of college can be as important to that student's sense of personal growth as the social adjustments students frequently need to make. This result is surprising, since most of the studies done on adjusting to college focus on nonacademic, co-curricular factors, such as adjusting to dorm life, finding friends, getting involved in college activities, and the like. The Terenzini/Wright study is surprising because it suggests that the academic reasons for being in college affect the personal growth patterns of college students.

Suggested Activities

1. Are Terenzini and Wright correct in their conclusion that academic adjustment is important to personal growth? Ask students to discuss the importance of academic studies to their college experience. Are they fitting in academically? How might the institution help them to fit in better or more quickly in academic ways?

2. Erickson and Strommer report that participation in co-curricular activities has declined on their campuses and nationally. Has that happened on your campus? Find the pamphlet or flyer that your institution publishes about the activities that students can join. Then have every student in your class select one of those activities to attend, participate in, and report about to the class as a whole. Once the reports have been made, invite students to discuss whether the array of available activities is appealing to them, and why--or why not. How can these experiences benefit them in the future (e.g., acquiring new skills, leadership opportunities, using them on a resume).

How Discrimination Works
and Why It Matters: Five Personal Statements

The five essays in this group are personal statements that report experiences with discrimination of several different kinds. Chana Schoenberger tells about a summer science camp she attended between her high school junior and senior years. There for the first time she met and interacted with people among whom her religion, Judaism, put her in a minority. She completed her essay and published it in <u>Newsweek</u> while she was still in high school.

The remaining four statements are by professional psychologists and counselors, and their shared academic training is evident in many ways as they discuss their sense of being different from the mainstream social norms that surround them. Joy Weeber reports experiences related to her physical disability, scoliosis. "Most of us with disabilities," she writes, "learn to survive alone and silent . . . never knowing a disability community exists." Edward Delgado-Romero talks about "covert . . . subtle racism that the victim of overt racism begins to internalize" as he recounts his father's reaction to majority thinking about his Spanish and Latin American roots. Donna Talbot, whose mother "is 100 percent Japanese," discussed her experiences as an Asian-American.

Finally, Lisa Brandyberry identifies herself as "poor, White, trash" and "fat." She tells about developing a sense of personal identity thanks to which she feels closer to a friend who is African-American and lesbian than to members of her white majority group. Brandyberry's essay is a somewhat surprising conclusion to this group of five. After discussing issues springing from race, class, body size, gender, and sexual orientation, Brandyberry explains how she became an "ally" in the struggles of minority groups and what this title has meant for her.

Discussion Questions

1.   What do these five essays have in common?

Each of these essays takes up a topic related to prejudice or intolerance, each of them points out the price that some individuals have had to pay as victims of prejudice, and each of them identifies a lesson for readers to act on in their own future behavior with respect to members of groups that have been targets of discrimination.

2.   Each of these essays considers diversity from a different kind of concern. Are they equally important concerns? If you had to rank them, how would you select the one or two that truly matter? If you find you cannot rank them in importance, why not?

This series of questions is meant to elicit value-laden discussions about the rights of various minorities to live free from the effects of discrimination and bigotry. If the criterion used to compare these instances is the personal cost of prejudice, then it will be very difficult to rank the suffering of the fat person who has been humiliated publicly, the Jewish student surprised and wounded by a careless word from a teacher, and the black student who has lost a good friend because of group behavior that imposes separation on individual members of racial or ethnic groups.

Is there more prejudice against blacks than, say, against Jews or fat people? Or is the prejudice that Jews witness in anti-Semitic bombings greater or less than what African-Americans see when black children are killed in the burning of a black church? Perhaps others can provide a rationale that defines degrees of suffering based on one specific kind of prejudice rather than another, but we cannot. Why not? Because identifying any one of these forms of prejudice as less important than another would itself be an act of prejudice: we would have to argue somehow that one of these groups does not feel the results of discrimination as deeply as the others do.

3.   Do these authors raise issues of political correctness? Or is that too narrow a way of viewing their experiences?

     None of these authors depends on "political correctness," but each of them calls on the reader to get involved and to change intolerant behaviors, including incautious words that wound members of the audience without the speaker being aware of doing so.

4.   What other groups--minority or majority--might put forward similar experiences and draw similar conclusions from them?

     Many groups have suffered from prejudicial opinions and actions about that group. When the Irish first immigrated to America in large groups, "Paddy" and "Mick" were derogatory terms used about them. Until John F. Kennedy won the office of President of the United States, Roman Catholics were publicly criticized as tools of the Pope who would sell out America to the Roman Catholic Church. In some colleges, students who join fraternities or sororities are smeared by that association, and on other campuses "independent students" (that is, non-"Greeks") are isolated and belittled. Just about any group that someone can join or be born into is likely to be someone else's target. Gays, Muslims, people from the South--the list is virtually endless.

5.   Federal, state, and local laws now identify specific groups of people as "protected classes." These usually include groups defined by characteristics shared in common such as religion, race, gender, physical disability, and Vietnam-era veteran status. Should these be legally "protected" classes? Explain.

     Here the discussion issues are likely to hinge the meaning of "legally protected." When legal protections are interpreted to mean requiring quotas or preferring unqualified candidates over qualified ones, then most students will argue against the notion of protected classes. But if legal protections are in place to insure a level playing field--that is, if the purpose of legally protected classes is to insure that everyone has an equal chance to let genuine merit be recognized and rewarded, most fair-minded students will not object.

Suggested Activities

1.   Ask students to list the groups with which they identify. In addition to the groups you have already discussed in class (such as racial groups, gender groups, fat people), suggest some groups that may not conventionally spring to mind--such as "teenagers," "fans of the Grateful Dead," "people from West Virginia," "members of the Jones family," "Italians," "athletes," "mathematicians," "fraternity members," "Methodists," "fans of the Cleveland Browns" and the like. (Students should be encouraged not to write the name of any group for which they might suffer or be embarrassed if their list falls into other hands.) Then ask students to underline any of the groups on their personal list that have been the target of discrimination. Once students have completed this exercise, you will have reminded them all—or virtually all--of occasions when they were personally hurt by someone else's prejudice. Ask students to write a brief essay about the effects of prejudice as they know them.

2.   Invite students to identify someone of a different race or cultural background with whom they have developed a close personal friendship. Then assign them to write a brief essay in which they discuss what this friendship taught them. If they cannot honestly identify such a cross-cultural friendship, ask them to write instead about what they could do to cross cultural barriers and form such a friendship.

Race and Racism in America
Jesse L. Jackson, Sr.

A recurring theme in this essay by the Reverend Jesse Jackson Sr. is that America's progress toward civil rights for all is rooted in individual acts of courage. Great outcomes for Americans in general result from recognizing that "race is not the issue, but that injustice is, and that for racism to stop, the injustices perpetrated by one side or the other must end." However, he says one lesson he learned in the Civil Rights Movement is that "although everyone has a responsibility to eliminate racism, a special responsibility rests with those who hold effective power." Jackson points to many ways in which the Civil Rights Movement has been good to America in general, even though, he contends, racism continues and must continually be opposed.

Discussion Questions

1. Jackson correctly points out that higher education has been at the center of much discussion about affirmative action. What is the current state of affirmative action laws in your state? Does race or other minority status have a place in admissions or other policies of your college? Should it?

   The answer to this question will, of course, vary by state and college. But two objectives should be part of the discussion related to this prompt. First, students should complete the discussion knowing about your university's major policies related to race, gender, sexual orientation, and related issues as they bear on their lives at your school. What are the penalties for sexual harassment? Who can they turn to if they have questions about those policies or wish to report a problem? Second, students should talk about the issues related to these policies. What is required by fairness? What do they think about policies that single out race or gender as a defining factor?

2. Do you consider yourself to be a member of a minority? If so, have you benefited from the civil rights movement in any way that you are aware of? Ask your parents or older friends to comment on this question, and check to see if your answer agrees with theirs.

   This question should be assigned in advance of class discussion. Students should be encouraged to talk with at least one "older" person—that is, with someone who lived through the experiences of the 1960s or 1970s in the United states and can make some eye-witness judgments. "Minority" can be taken to cover more than the usual categories, but students might want to talk with the teacher in advance for any group about which they may feel uncertain.

3. Jackson points to a demographic fact that is widely acknowledged—namely, within your lifetime there will be no majority population in the United states. How will this affect your life in the future? How should you plan for that now?

   You may well find that some students in your class already live in such an environment. Students from many large cities of the South will report that no ethnic group encompasses half or more of the population of their hometown. Start by asking them to describe the groups there and how they fit in. Other students may report that they attended a high school that changed demographically during their time in it, or perhaps they have friends from a minority group who can tell them a little about what it is like to live **not** in the majority group.

Suggested Activity

Does your campus or community have a speakers bureau with persons who will come to your class to talk about the issues in this essay? If so, invite a gay man or a lesbian to come to class and tell his or her own story, or invite students to argue for or against bringing an openly gay speaker to class. (If you do plan to invite a speaker, be sure to check your school's policies on inviting guest speakers.)

I Have a Dream
Martin Luther King, Jr.

We close Unit 8 with Dr. Martin Luther King's 1963 speech to the participants in the March on Washington for Civil Rights, which, thanks to its closing sequence of increasingly fervent visions, is generally known as "I Have a Dream." A masterpiece of oratorical art, this exhortation calls upon America to make good on the promise of the ideals voiced by the framers of the <u>Declaration of Independence</u> and of the <u>Constitution</u>--to make good on the claim that all men are created equal, to deliver on the promise of full emancipation proclaimed by Abraham Lincoln one hundred years earlier.

King urges his audience to work toward those ideals in nonviolent ways when they return to their homes throughout the United States, "with the faith that unearned suffering is redemptive." Then he describes his vision of a world in which the American ideals of equality and equal justice for all have come truly into being.

We close with this selection because the ideals that King celebrates and hopes to see become reality are also the ideals of the college or university--especially, the ideal <u>American</u> college or university. King weaves together the language of his Christian faith and the language of great voices in America's past to call the nation to remember the values which gave America its birth. These values and the protections that they promise to individuals are consistent with the ideals that define a college or university, where all ideas are accorded an equal hearing, where judgments are based only on the merit of those ideas.

Discussion Questions

1. What does King mean by the phrase, "the tranquilizing drug of gradualism"?

    King is saying that justice is not achieved by slow degrees. A policy or an action is either just or it is not just, so promises of a gradual transition to justice--"We can't make these changes all at once. We need to go slowly. Let's do the right thing a little at a time"--are merely delaying tactics used by those in power to tranquilize the people suffering injustice.

2. King argues that physical force must be countered by "soul force." What does he mean?

    It is well known that King respected and followed the example of Mahatma Gandhi in implementing revolution through nonviolent means. Gandhi showed that an unshakable belief in the moral rightness of a cause is stronger than armies. On this issue the great religious traditions of both East and West converge. King also meant that wrongful means cannot lead to a righteous end.

3. Using the language of his own time, King speaks of "the Negro." Today's authors would probably not use this word. Why?

    Language is dynamic. The student of the history of language can point to many examples of how the connotative elements of language change. For example, in English we use many words to refer to human females, and those words carry very different meanings ("female," "woman," "lady," "girl," and "chick," to provide only a few). As times and contexts change, these words may move from carrying positive connotations to neutral to negative. Many authors who would currently choose "female" as a neutral word for "woman" once would have preferred "woman" and, years earlier, "lady."

"Colored person," "Negro," "Black," "Afro-American," "African American," and "person of color" are all variant terms that apply to the same race (though "person of color" is more general in that it includes all non-white races). Each of these terms has in its turn, for some part of the last century, been the preferred polite usage. In 1963, King would have sounded old-fashioned and somewhat patronizing to speak of "the colored person"; he would have alienated some of his audience if he had used the term "Black," which in 1963 sounded more radical than King may have wanted to be on this special occasion; and his audience would have stumbled over terms like "Afro-American" and "African American," which were not yet in general use.

4. Discuss the ways in which repetition of key words and phrases plays a part in making this an effective speech.

    Much of the power of King's speech arises out of the way he uses language to support his call for nonviolent action to bring about his vision of a just American society. To understand how language functions in this speech, students should read and reread the speech looking for King's methods of building from his opening observations to the grand rolling sentences of his final paragraphs. On the skeleton of a relatively simple outline, King marks out the sections of his argument by using repetition of key words and phrases within a section, then moving to a new repeated element for his next major thought. Examples include his use of "one hundred years later," "promissory note," "now is the time," "we can never be satisfied," "go back to . . . ," "I have a dream," and "Let freedom ring."

5. As a Christian minister, King drew heavily on the language of the Bible, which was natural to him. What effect does including such language ("we will not be satisfied until justice rolls down like waters and righteousness like a mighty stream," "every valley shall be exalted, every hill and mountain shall be made low") add to this speech?

    When we hear King's use of Biblical language, we almost inevitably also feel the spiritual connotations of that language. King's argument is enhanced by the authority inherent in the sound of a prophet who believes that he is speaking at the direction of God. As a protestant minister, King spoke with the authority of someone ordained to a religious life, especially when he consciously evoked the image of the righteous prophet addressing the multitude. That rhetorical stance and the religious imagery used to develop it set his speech into a context that King knew well, that many in his audience fervently believed, and that supported the affect he wished to have on those who heard him.

Suggested Activities

1. Theories of student development usually treat the process of development as a gradual one, following stages that depend on maturity and the accumulation of experience. But sometimes our development happens much more dramatically, and we can ever after identify the day or even the moment that we discovered something that changed our thinking and our behavior. Sometimes that thing affects an entire generation and moves it into a new direction.

    Ask students to identify a single thing--perhaps a song, a book, a film, an event like the concert at Woodstock--that affected them powerfully and permanently, in the way that the March on Washington and Martin Luther King's speech galvanized and changed hundreds of thousands of people, virtually all at once. Ask them to write a brief essay that focuses on that single motivating force or event and to explain its influence. How does the "Million Man March" of today compare with the "March on Washington" in the 1960's?

2.   Has King's dream of equal justice for all become reality? Ask students to evaluate the progress of civil rights for all Americans as they have seen it. What goals have been accomplished? What steps need to be taken next?

UNIT 9

LIFE AFTER COLLEGE: FUTURE SUCCESS OR FUTURE SHOCK?

The theme for the last group of essays is one that many beginning students don't consider too seriously when they begin college--that of preparing for the day they will leave the comparative safety of campus life and venture into the work world as a college graduate. The essays are also about many of the issues discussed in the first unit about the value of a college degree and the reasons for engaging in the college experience. Now, however, the emphasis is on how to use their knowledge and skills in the environment for which they have been preparing. As these essays are discussed in class, referring to the readings in the other units can add deeper insights to the many ideas and suggestions the previous essay authors have provided. Another theme that pervades this last unit is goal-setting. The readings in Unit 9 ask students to consider the future and what type of person they want to become during their college years. Goal-setting, therefore, can become an important topic in class discussion and in assignments.

UNIT 9 READINGS

Having a Degree and Being Educated
Edmund D. Pellegrino, M.D.

This essay was first delivered as an address at commencement. In it Pellegrino challenges students to think about the difference between "having a degree and being educated." In Unit 1, several essays described an "educated person." How does Pellegrino define the educated person in this essay? He talks about some of the ills of society and how educated people can help resolve some of these problems.

Discussion Questions

1.   Why does Dr. Pellegrino think it is an illusion that having a degree and being educated are the same?

Having a degree signifies that students have absorbed many ideas, facts, and information about a great many subjects. Being educated means that they have learned how to use the information in ways beyond its narrow confines. How one's mind operates is the mark of an educated person.

2.   What is an underduated person, according to Pellegrino?

One who cannot separate his or her opinions from another's thinking. One who cannot answer questions of truth and justice for themselves. One who has not learned to grapple with the "kind of question that separates humans from animals and computers." How would students define an "uneducated person"? Does one need a college degree to learn this higher order of thinking?

3.   How does Pellegrino define knowledge?

Knowledge is "recognition of something absent," a beginning, not an end. It is not enough to have gathered information, but we need to determine "how we should use this knowledge, whether we should use it, and for what purposes." Is this a satisfactory definition of knowledge for the students? What has been their definition of the word? How is it different or the same as Pellegrino's?

4.   List six ways that, according to Pellegrino, the mind works. Why?

The six ways include have they learned to learn, can they ask critical questions, can they understand all the nuances of their own language, are their actions their own, can they form reasoned judgments about the arts, and are their political opinions based on their own conclusions? These six are the "essence of a liberal education," one that indicates they are in control of their own thinking.

5.   What are the two kinds of freedom needed to live "truly human lives," according to Pellegrino?

One is political and the other intellectual and spiritual. Each depends on the other. Can the students speculate what it would be like to be deprived of these freedoms? What has happened in other countries when these freedoms have been denied?

Suggested Activities

1.   Ask students to write their own essay on the topic Pellegrino proposes: In their own view, what is the difference between having a degree and being educated?

2.   Ask students to take the six questions about being "educated" and answer them in the context of their own present situation. If they cannot answer yes to any, how might they use their college experience to ensure they will be able to say "yes" at graduation?

Peering into the Future with Wilbur and Orville Wright
Malcolm Wells

Wells' spoof, a mythical conversation between the Wright brothers, makes a statement about how important it is to think about the future with an open and creative mind. Wilbur represents a thinker who only sees the future from his own narrow perspective while Orville thinks "out of the box" to envision a future that no one could imagine at that time in history. Although students will enjoy this reading because of its humor, hopefully they will also understand how in this technological age we need to think about the future with open minds and creative imaginations.

Discussion Questions

1. How does the author use humor to help you think about the future?

   This conversation is based on a question that Wilbur Wright actually posed about the future of the airplane. Wells' use of humor helps make his point more emphatically. No matter how crazy or far out future predictions may seem, being open to new ideas can create an environment where anything is possible.

2. Can you imagine such a conversation actually taking place in the Wright Brother's era? Why or why not? Could it take place now, but related to some other miracle of modern engineering? Why or why not?

   The substance of this conversation probably did take place in the Wright Brother's time. As described in the Zuckerman essay in Unit 5, many of the inventions that changed life dramatically in the last century appeared at about the same time as the first flight. Futurists from many areas of society continue to make outlandish predictions for the future, some of which will undoubtedly come true as some of Orville's did in this reading. Without persistence and creative thinking on the part of people like the Wright Brothers, technological progress would probably not have advanced as it did.

3. Wilbur insists on viewing the future based on what he knows in his own time. How does this affect his ability to imagine the future and its possibilities?

   Looking at the future from the narrow perspective of our current experiences and knowledge limits our potential for thinking about innovative and creative ways of solving old problems or inventing new perspectives on old ideas.

4. In this brief selection, Orville proves himself to be a futurist. What characteristics do you think are necessary for becoming a futurist?

   There are probably as many characteristics as there are futurists, but many have an expert knowledge of their field, an appreciation for the history of that field, and the ability to think beyond what is logical or reasonable. Futurists probably need an almost child-like imagination, not allowing any restriction or limit to their thoughts about what is possible.

Suggested Activity

Ask students to create a similar dialogue between Alexander Graham Bell and Watson while testing the telephone. How would these two inventors describe the technology that allows us to talk to each other today without wires?

A Time of Discontinuity
Arthur Levine and Jeanette S. Cureton

After providing a brief historical perspective on the history of society, the authors describe the current time and how college students are affected by the events taking place. This reading, from their book *When Hope and Fear Collide*, is the conclusion to a study the authors did for the Carnegie Council to obtain a profile of current college students. Sharing other aspects of the book with students may help to broaden their understanding of how today's world is different from that of past generations' and why their future will be very different from that faced by their parents and grandparents.

Discussion Questions

1. According to the authors, what are the two periods in history when profound change occurred? What do these two periods have in common?

   The authors describe the Industrial Revolution as a period of profound change when society was transformed from an agricultural to an industrial society. The second time of profound change is now, according to Levine and Cureton. Demographic, economic, global, and technological changes are occurring at a rapid pace.

2. Why do the authors claim the benefit of a college education has diminished?

   The benefit of a college education has diminished because of the enormous size of the population attending college. College graduates, who in the past were a small minority, are no longer the elite who can be sheltered from the social forces that protected them from rapid change in the past.

3. Do you agree with the authors' description of current undergraduates? Why or why not?

   Students may agree with all or some of the characteristics the authors list. An interesting discussion can evolve from comparing those characteristics that seem to most closely resemble the students on your campus.

4. What four attributes must a college education provide? Do you agree these are the most important for the future? Why or why not?

   Hope, responsibility, appreciation of differences, and efficacy are the four attributes of an education that must exist in order to insure that this generation of college students will realize their dreams and be leaders of society. Students may not agree that these are the *most* important attributes, but probably they will acknowledge they are vital to their future.

5. What can college students do to make sure they will "make a difference"?

   First, they will need to believe that they *can* make a difference in every life they touch. Some students, however, may not believe that it is their responsibility to make a difference or that they owe anything to others. A discussion about what they owe society or what society "owes" them will provide an opportunity for them to share different points of view on the subject.

Suggested Activities

1. Ask students to generate their own list of characteristics that describe today's traditional-age college students. How is it different from the authors' list in this reading? Discuss the implications of these characteristics as they will affect the future of society.

2. If you have worked with students on a college campus for some time, share your views of how these students are the same or different from other generations you have experienced.

Outlooks and Insights: Succeeding on the Job and in Life
Carol Carter

We end this unit with a reading that offers advice in a positive way about some of the issues students will face as they begin life after college. Carter discusses the uniqueness of individuals, ethical behavior, happiness, and how to prepare for the day after graduation.

Discussion Questions

1.   How is your first job like a blank page, according to Carter?

It is like a blank page because "you fill it in as you go." At this stage your opportunities are unlimited and are what you make of them. Have students ever thought of their first job as a "blank page"?

2.   Do you agree that many measurements of success that people use only have to do with "appearances"? Explain.

Discussion can encourage students to define "success." Does "being a successful person" mean the same to everyone? Appearances reflect what people want others to think about them; it does not necessarily indicate what they really are. No amount of money or possessions, according to Carter, can make you happy if you are not comfortable with who you are. Do students agree with this premise?

3.   What are some "games people play"?

They are constantly comparing themselves to others. They value material things and try to impress other people with their possessions. They may feel threatened by who you are and try to pull you down. Can students describe some other games that insecure people play?

4.   Why is ethical behavior so important in the workplace?

People and organizations need to set standards for individual and collective behavior. Without ethical behavior, there would be a "no-holds barred," free-for-all atmosphere that would not further the common good. Knowing right from wrong is critical in any pursuit. What is the students' understanding of ethical behavior? Does it change in different situations? How does it pertain to the college environment? Referring back to Unit 7 can help review some of the ethical principles discussed there.

5.   Why is it important to balance your personal and professional life?

One stimulates the other and encourages renewal of our source of energy. Are there people who do not need this balance? How do people get ahead in today's demanding world without sacrificing some aspect of their life?

Suggested Activities

1. Ask students to write about what they would like to accomplish on their first job. First, they might fantasize about what it will be, and then describe what they hope will happen to them. For older students, ask them to think about their first job and what they would do if they could start all over. How did they fill in their blank page? Were they happy with the results?

2.   Suggest students read the book from which this essay is taken, *Majoring in the Rest of Your Life*. What other advice do Carter and the other authors give for making the most out of a college career?

ADDITIONAL READINGS FOR INSTRUCTORS

Astin, A.W., (1993). *What matters in college?* San Francisco: Jossey-Bass.

Barefoot, B.O. (Ed.)(1993). *Exploring the evidence: reporting outcomes of freshman seminars* (Monograph No. 11). Columbia, SC: University of South Carolina, National Resource Center for The Freshman Year Experience.

Barefoot, B.O., & Fidler, P. (1991). *National survey of freshman seminar programming* (Monograph No. 10). Columbia, SC: University of South Carolina, National Resource Center for The Freshman Year Experience.

Border, L.B., & Chism, N.V.C. (Eds.)(1992). *Teaching for diversity.* San Francisco: Jossey-Bass.

Boyer, E.L. (1987). *College: The undergraduate experience in America.* New York: Harper & Row.

Chickering, A.W., & Reisser, L. (1993). *Education and identity (2nd Edition).* San Francisco: Jossey-Bass.

Chickering, A. W. & Associates (1981). *The modern American college.* San Francisco: Jossey-Bass.

Erickson, B.L., & Strommer, D. (1991). *Teaching college freshmen.* San Francisco: Jossey-Bass.

Fitts, C.T., & Swift, F.H. (1928). The construction of orientation courses for college freshmen. *University of California Publications in Education.* 1897-1929, 2. 145-250.

Gabelnick, F., MacGregor, J., Matthews, B.S., & Smith, B.L. (1990). Learning communities: Creating connections among students, faculty and disciplines. *New Directions for Teaching and Learning.* No. 41. San Francisco: Jossey-Bass.

Gordon, V.N. (1989). Origins and purposes of the freshman seminar. In M.L. Upcraft & J. N. Gardner (Eds.), *The freshman year experience: Helping students survive and succeed in college (pp.* 261-276). San Francisco: Jossey-Bass

Katchadourian, H.A., & Boli, J. (1985). *Careerism and intellectualism among college students.* San Francisco: Jossey-Bass.

Keefe, J.W. (Ed.)(1988). *Profiling and utilizing learning style.* Reston, VA: National Association of Secondary School Principals.

Kiersey, D., & Bates, M. (1978). *Please understand me: character and temperament types.* Del Mar, CA: Prometheus Nemesis Books.

King, M.D.(Ed.)(1993). Academic advising: Organizing and delivering services for student success. *New Directions for Community Colleges.* No. 82. San Francisco: Jossey-Bass.

Kuh, G.D., Schuh, J.H., & Witt, E.J. (1991). *Involving colleges.* San Francisco: Jossey-Bass.

Levine, A (1985). *Handbook of undergraduate curriculum.* San Francisco: Jossey-Bass.

Mayhew, L., Ford, P., & Hubbard, D. (1990). *The quest for quality: The challenge for undergraduate education in the 1990's.* San Francisco: Jossey-Bass.

McKeachie, W.J., Pintrich, P.R., Lin, Y., & Smith, D.A.F. (1990). *Teaching and learning in the classroom: A review of the literature (2nd ed).* Ann Arbor: University of Michigan.

Pascarella, E.T., & Terenzini, P.T. (1991). *How college affects students.* San Francisco: Jossey-Bass.

Perry, W.G., Jr. (1970). *Forms of intellectual and ethical development in the college years.* New York: Holt, Rinehart and Winston.

Reinarz, A.G., & White, E.R. (1995). Teaching through academic advising: A faculty perspective. *New Directions for Teaching and Learning,* No. 62. San Francisco: Jossey-Bass.

Tinto, V. (1994). Leaving college: *Rethinking the causes and cures of student attrition (2nd. ed).* Chicago, IL: The University of Chicago Press.

Upcraft, M.L. & Gardner, J.N. (Eds.)(1989). *The freshman year experience: Helping students survive and succeed in college.* San Francisco: Jossey-Bass.

Upcraft, M.L., & Kramer, G.L. (Eds.)(1995). *First year advising: Patterns in the present, pathways to the future.* (Monograph No. 18). Columbia, SC: National Resource Center for the Freshman Year Experience and the National Academic Advising Association.